THEORIES OF HOMOSEXUALITY

Martin Dannecker was born in 1942, and worked as a salesperson and actor before studying psychology. He was involved in the West German gay liberation movement from its beginnings, and in 1970 wrote the script for Rosa von Praunheim's film *It's Not the Homosexual that's Perverted, But the Society in Which He Lives*. Together with Reimut Reiche, he conducted a wide ranging survey of gay men in West Germany, published in 1974 as *The Average Homosexual*. He now teaches and researches in the Sexual Science Department of Frankfurt University.

Martin Dannecker

Theories of Homosexuality

GAY
MEN'S
PRESS

English edition first published 1981 by Gay Men's Press.
Copyright ©1978 Syndikat Autoren- and Verlagsgesellschaft,
Frankfurt am Main, West Germany.
Translation by David Fernbach ©1981 Gay Men's Press,
27 Priory Avenue, London N8 7RN.

**British Library/Library of Congress
Cataloguing in Publication Data**

Dannecker, Martin
  Theories of homosexuality.
  1. Homosexuality.
  I. Title   II. Der Homosexuelle und die
  Homosexualität. *English*
  306.7'6   HQ76

  ISBN 0 907040 05 5

Cover by Aubrey Walter
Photoset by Shanta Thawani, 25 Natal Road, London N11 2HL

Preface to the English Edition   7

Preface to the German Edition   12

1. Legalisation and Oppression   15

2. Homosexuality and Anthropology   25

3. The Biologising of Ethics   31

4. An Alternative Anthropology   33

5. Hirschfeld's Debate with Psychoanalysis   39

6. The Reduction of Homosexuality
to the Homosexual   44

7. Psychoanalysis versus Sexology   46

8. Anthropological Psychiatry   50

9. The Wave of Liberalism   55

10. The Popular 'Attitude' to Homosexuals   61

11. The Specific Homosexual Biography   67

12. Deviance and Social Adaptation   80

13. Homosexuality as a Psychological
Phenomenon   86

14. The Superior Homosexual   101

Notes   105

For Rüdiger

Preface to the English Edition

I am aware that this book may raise more questions than it solves, though I don't see this as a fault. It intentionally set out to provoke a debate, the reason being that I found so many answers given to the questions posed by homosexuality far too glib and simple. This was particularly so in the light of the empirical survey of gay men in West Germany that I carried out together with Reimut Reiche. The results of this were published in 1974 under the title *The Average Homosexual*.[1] But for all the data we accumulated, we deliberately left aside the question of etiology, and did not pursue the age-old and in general highly ideological concern with the causes of homosexuality which has so strikingly obsessed most past research.

The present book does begin to discuss this question, though in no way with the perspective that homosexuality is a sickness to be cured. In this discussion I place myself in the basic tradition of psychoanalysis, even though many psychoanalysts are themselves trapped in the ideas of a homophobic society. It is not surprising that there is an increasing tendency among homosexuals, especially those involved in the gay liberation movement, to view anything psychological, or even psychoanalytic, in an extremely hostile light. But it would be very hard to understand homosexuality and homosexuals without drawing on the findings of psychoanalysis. There always have been psychoanalysts, moreover, and they are a growing number today, who in no way pursue the ridiculous goal of doing away with homosexuality through therapy, but seek instead to treat a homosexual patient on the basis of his homosexuality.

From this allegiance to psychoanalysis, I take issue with the current fashion for 'labelling theory' or the 'labelling approach'. Here the problems that beset gay people are analysed simply in terms of social stigma: both the immediate kind, and the less direct kind that is built into the general social climate. I would not deny the relevance of the factors on which labelling theory focuses its attention. But its analysis does not go sufficiently deep, and I believe the theory and practice of psychoanalysis is needed if we are to get to the roots of homophobic violence and work to counter these. One thing this means is that we should stop denying those differences between homosexuals and heterosexuals that arise from a different structuring of erotic drives. Yet in the labelling approach I do perceive such a tendency to deny the differences between a homosexual and a heterosexual structure. I believe this denial is extremely damaging for homosexuals themselves, because the tacit but implicit demand is made that they should ultimately behave in the ways expected of them by the present society's ideas of social normality. And in the present society I am deeply convinced that homosexuals behave as they do because they are indeed different from the average heterosexual in a far deeper sense than that which the labelling approach discusses.

Where such distinctions can be seen and traced, I in no way see them as a fault. Nor can I see anything negative even when the average homosexual is or seems less well adapted than the average heterosexual. Adaptation as such is no virtue, especially in a society governed not by human needs but by the interests of capital. Both in Germany and elsewhere there is an automatic tendency to try and explain everything that seems strange, bizarre and immoral in homosexual behaviour, when measured according to what society sees as normal, desirable and moral, in terms of social persecution. But this strikes me as an unconsidered acceptance of a culture which cannot tolerate that anyone or anything should deviate from its horrific standards. I have pointed out this more or less hidden tendency at work in research into homosexuality, and argued that the attitude of depriving homosexuals of their specific difference has actually increased, when seen in historical perspective. Despite surface appearance, the response to homosexuals today is far removed from genuine tolerance and acceptance. Any tolerance that really deserves this name respects what is different on its own terms, and in no way seeks to obliterate its different aspect. Yet attempts of this kind are especially characteristic of American research.

The French theory of homosexuality, as represented for example by Guy Hocquenghem, takes a markedly different tack, and one that I find more sympathetic. My criticism of it bears simply on its anthropologisation of present-day gay men. I share however its view that homosexuality represents a component of human drive that is so far unliberated. If this component is suppressed, as is normally the case with heterosexuals, this leads to a specific construction of the personality. If it alone is allowed expression, on the other hand, as is normally the case with homosexuals, then we are also faced with a specific construction. It is heterosexual lunacy to view what is specific about homosexuality as pathological. Once this lunatic view is abandoned, then the specific lines of homosexual development, its possibilities and abilities, in short everything that is different about it, can not only be presented as they are. It also becomes possible to accept this difference on its own terms.

Most previous research on homosexuality, including research with good intentions, failed to do justice to homosexuals in as much as it was governed by a view centred on heterosexuality. The traditional research, without being aware of it, never abandoned a view in which sexuality was equated with heterosexuality, for ostensibly 'obvious' reasons. Paradoxically, this was also true of those works which stand out because they do not betray from the very start a discriminatory attitude. Whenever they had occasion to deal with those aspects of homosexuality that are different, they reacted in the same disturbed fashion as 19th century anthropologists who encountered 'savages'. These early explorers were only able to deal with their irritation at people who were different and strange in the terms provided by their own culture. This palpable irritation at the specific forms of behaviour characteristic of homosexuals strikes me as indicating the degree to which research into homosexuality identifies with the heterosexual norm. The example I have chosen in this short book is promiscuity, which in so many studies is either excluded or denied because it is scarcely compatible, if at all, with the pattern that the heterosexual norm hammers into people's heads.

I should like to note, by way of self-criticism, that I may myself have succeeded less than completely in raising my sights to an immanent analysis of the homosexual world, analysing it in its own perspective and according to its specific laws. I may myself have got drawn in here and there to viewing homosexuality from the angle of heterosexuality. If so, this must be put down to the strong compulsion of the prescribed normality. An indication of this would be any presentation of the homosexual world as in some sense disordered. It is in no way disordered, but it is in many somewhat subtle ways different from the world habitually considered normal.

I should like to conclude on the question of homosexual love. Despite the importance I attach to this, it is clear that homosexual relationships cannot be measured with the same standard applied to heterosexual mariage. I am certainly convinced that homosexuals can have happy, passionate and lasting relationships. Yet here too the specific character of these relationships should be borne in mind. What makes for happiness here tends to be somewhat different from the case of the traditional couple. The desired 'lasting' quality of the relationship, which need not be permanent, involves rather a mutual understanding of the basic difficulties that can erupt in a love relationship, an understanding that does not stop short when faced with 'sexual infidelity', i.e. the tendency to promiscuity. But this means ceasing to identify with the traditional ideas of love and fidelity.

One reason why we must distance ourselves from these traditional ideas, and not the least reason either, is that the drama of sexuality is not as intense among homosexuals as among heterosexuals, or at least this has been the case up till now. What I mean by this drama is that passion has no place defined by moral custom. Within marriage, passion has to adjust to domestication. Passionate sexuality and marriage do not fit well together, and there is good reason why the great bourgeois novels place passion outside of marriage. It could only be had at the price of immorality. Passion was epitomised in the life of Effi Briest or Emma Bovary, and here it takes the sense of suffering. But if passionate love is equated with suffering, this lies less in the nature of love than in the moral framework of society, which allows no room for passion of any kind. And not only the heroines of bourgeois fiction, but gay men too, still bear witness to this fact today.

Frankfurt, April 1981

Preface to the German Edition

Even before this book was published, it met with a reaction I had feared in the course of writing. After seeing a copy of the typescript, the spokesperson for a gay liberation group pressed me most strongly not to take part in a radio programme on which I had been invited to appear. The history of this book explains why I could anticipate such a violent reaction. Until not very long ago I was myself actively involved in the 'second' homosexual movement, and could even say I was one of its leaders. Much that was discussed at that time, and much that was not voiced but was tacitly present, has found its way into the present text, though without being explicitly referred to. I should therefore like to thank everyone who I discussed things with in the course of those years. These were the people who led me to write this book, even if they were unaware of it.

There were two reasons for fearing a hostile reaction. Though I hoped this would not happen, I suspected that sections of the gay movement would simply reject the book as erroneous, without any serious debate. Yet it was written by someone who in no way stands outside the things he writes about, but right in the midst of them. And so my fear also had a second and directly personal aspect, i.e. of being treated as a miscreant by a movement to which I could not be indifferent.

I should also mention here a further response, more in the direction I had hoped for. There are signs of the beginning of a debate with those theses in it that are especially explosive for homosexuals, a debate which Rüdiger Lautmann has started with his book *Society and Homosexuality*[1]. The hope that a debate of this kind is possible, and my conviction that it is needed, helped me to write this text and encouraged me to publish it.

In the present book I have taken up ideas that were mentioned only in passing in the study I published together with Reimut Reiche, *The Average Homosexual*. These bear mainly on the question of what it is that is different about the male homosexual and his milieu. In that connection I had more to learn than Reimut Reiche, and I found a lot of questions I had still to work through. Reimut's comment after reading the present text, that we had said all this before, is true in so far as we had indeed discussed many of the ideas presented here. Yet for various reasons, in particular the empirical character of *The Average Homosexual*, we had not expressed these thoughts in print. For this reason alone, it will be clear what a debt I owe to Reimut Reiche. Our empirical work together remains the basis for the present text. This is as it were its continuation, even if in a different form.

Frankfurt, December 1977

1. Legalisation and Oppression

In 1962 the Christian-Democrat government of West Germany proposed a new criminal code that maintained the 'general penalisation' of homosexuality. The only change was to be the abolition of the severer additions that the Nazis had made in 1935 to paragraph 175, which had been part of the German criminal code since 1871. In the wake of this proposal, a new discussion flared up around the 'criminality' of homosexuality.[1] The windy arguments put forward for the proposal particularly met with sharp rejection. T. Brocher diagnosed an ignorance of the 'results of scientific investigation'.[2] A. Mergen censured the recourse to 'healthy popular sentiment', which was how the federal government dealt with the objection 'that in a democratic social order the legislature should only impose a penalty if the action in question is injurious to a right that requires protection'.[3]

The rejection of this proposal by liberal critics was so unanimous because the federal government had backed up its case with arguments that echoed both in form and content the fascist propaganda calling for the extermination of homosexuals. In 1936, Himmler had proclaimed the impending mass murder of homosexuals in the following terms: 'Just as we have today found our way back to the old-Germanic view on the question of miscegenation between different races, so we must similarly return in our judgement of the race-destroying and degenerate phenomenon of homosexuality to the moral idea of eliminating the degenerate.'[4] According to the witchhunting booklet of Rudolf Klare,[5] the 'elimination of the degenerate' was necessary because 'homosexual behaviour injures the highest right of nation and state to keep pure the blood-values of the people'.[6] Of course, as Günther Gollner comments on the fascist ideology of blood-and-soil, 'this concern for the purity of the race failed to indicate any causal nexus between social values and homosexuality, since there is no way of showing how homosexuals can affect the "blood-substance" of the people, given that they are generally excluded from procreation'.[7] Certainly, this fascist ideology lacked a causal connection. Yet we may well ask whether a criticism at this level is not too superficial for so monstrous an allegation.

What governs and pervades Klare's writing is homophobia, the hatred of homosexuals. This is all that holds it together, and it does so in such a blatant fashion that there is no need to pick its logic to pieces. Yet even such a madness can have method in it, as is shown by a controversy on the 'homosexual question' that broke out in 1940-41 between a psychiatrist and an endocrinologist. At the centre of this debate was the old argument as to whether homosexuality was a biological or a psychological phenomenon. This was not something of mere theoretical interest, but a question of extreme practical relevance, 'of decisive importance for population policy'.[8] In his reply to an article by Paul Schröder, who had rejected the thesis of 'innate inversion', T. Lang wrote:

> The exclusion of homosexuals from procreation should be seen from the perspective of qualitative as well as quantitative population policy. If, as is not improbable, most cases of homosexuality arise from a chromosomic disturbance, then a severe prosecution and moral proscription which drives homosexuals to

at least attempt marriage and procreation will achieve the very opposite of its intended purpose, i.e. an actual increase in the number of homosexuals (and possibly also an increased number of physical deformities or prenatal mortalities) in subsequent generations.[9]

Since legal prosecution was not attenuated, homosexuals allegedly presented, according to this argument, a danger to one of the 'substantive values' of Nazi 'right', i.e. fighting power.[10] As far as the practical solution of the 'homosexual question' was concerned, this could only mean, and particularly in wartime, what Klare had already defined some years previously as the purpose of criminalisation: the punishment of homosexuals aimed 'neither at deterrence, nor retaliation, nor cure, but at the *temporary or permanent exclusion of the inverts from the community*',[11] the ultimate meaning of this being nothing less than incarceration and extermination in the concentration camps.

In order to show how the argument put forward for the 1962 penal code agrees in essentials with the Nazi argument, it is only necessary to compare key sentences from the two documents. There is no need for any commentary here, as the sole purpose is to show, behind a certain clean-up of vocabulary, the strikingly identical way in which homosexuality and homosexuals are treated. And moreover, both the proposed legislation of 1962 (hereafter referred to as E62) and Klare's fascist propaganda text do not confine themselves to a justification of their moral judgements and anthropological ideas, but extend similarly into the realm of fantasy.

Looking back at the Weimar republic and the attempts at that time to decriminalise homosexuality, Klare plays off the people against the intellectuals. The supporters of legalising homosexuality had never succeeded in 'finding a response among the broad strata of our people — despite the ever firmer support they obtained in certain intellectual circles'.[12] In similar vein, the argument for E62 counterposes the 'circles directly interested'[13] in the abolition of paragraph 175, or sometimes simply the 'interested circles'[14], to the 'overwhelming opinion of the population'[15], or the 'overwhelming view of the *German* population'.[16]

The upshot of this loose attitude to the penal code in the Weimar republic, Klare maintained, was 'a terrifying increase in homosexual activity, especially among the young, which could not but present a danger for people, state and race, unless it was halted by the ruthless vigour and determination of the law'.[17] And for E62, it was incontestable that 'the purity and health of sexual life is a precondition of extraordinary importance for the stability of the people and the preservation of the natural order of life, and our growing young people in particular require express protection from moral danger'.[18]

This coincidence of views also obtains in respect of the paranoic treatment of history, and here E62 could actually claim to outdo Klare in its language. Klare: 'History teaches us that a state is committed to decay if it does not counter the spread of homosexual practices with decisive counter-measures'.[19] E62: 'Wherever homosexual vice has taken hold and become widespread, the consequence has always been the degeneration of the people and the decay of its moral powers'.[20]

Where Klare speaks of 'Nordic-Germanic sentiment' which demands 'punishment for homosexual activity', [21] the 1962 draft prefers to talk of the 'healthy and natural order of life among the people'.[22]

It would be easy to find further examples to show the identical arguments that E62 shared with Nazi ideology.[23] Yet it is significant that the objections raised against E62 did not introduce any considerations going beyond legal discrimination. This was actually a deliberate choice made by the advocates of homosexual legalisation. Strange as it may now seem, they hoped that by shunning any depiction or analysis of the social position of homosexuals they could avoid fanning still further the flames of irrationality expressed in E62. The social position of homosexuals, accordingly, only came into the picture where there was an intended or actual connection with their special treatment by the law. This however reinforced the impression that a modification of the criminal code would more or less automatically bring with it a positive improvement in homosexual life. By reducing the debate to the law and its consequences, not only was the life situation of homosexuals reduced to the aspect of criminalisation, but this also contributed to repressing from consciousness the general homophobic structures in West Germany. Because discrimination and antipathy were only discussed in terms of the criminal law, the impression was given that the problem would be ended once the law was changed.

The longer the debate around the irrationality of criminal penalties continued, the more the actual homosexual disappeared from view. What was problematic and in need of change in the social position of homosexuals was reduced to the single issue of criminality. Ultimately, this abstraction from the overall context of homosexual life led to the widespread idea that the absence of discriminatory legislation was identical with a positive tolerance. That homosexuals were themselves affected by ideas of this kind, and fixed their attention too rigidly on the penal code, can be seen from an article by Thorsten Graf and Mimi Steglitz in 1974. They perceived on all sides a decline in the taboo on homosexuality, which they attributed to a powerful 'tendency to the integration of homosexuals':[24] 'One of the most striking results of the tendency to reduce the additional oppression of homosexuals is perhaps to be seen in the repeal of anti-homosexual legislation in a whole series of capitalist countries. . .'[25]

There can be no doubt that anti-homosexual legislation is a massive instrument of homosexual oppression. Yet it is in no way the only one, and possibly not even the most effective link in the chain of anti-homosexual measures. In fact, anti-homosexual laws are only a very partial index of the social position of homosexuals and the level of social tolerance, since normative legal prescriptions cannot be equated with objective right: 'To assert the objective existence of law, it is not enough to know its normative content, rather one must know too whether this normative content materialises in life, that is in social relations.'[26] Legal norms can be undermined and deprived of content by changed social relations, which may also mean in practice that legal sanctions are not imposed, or are imposed only in a more limited context. Thus the general uncertainty of the position before the modification of paragraph 175 tended to anticipate the partial liberalisation conceded in 1969. This led to a legal practice in which extremely different penalties were imposed for the same 'severity' of offence: 'Some judges impose substantial terms of imprisonment, others only a small fine. It is apparent from the arguments given that the penalties here are highly dependent on the subjective attitude of the judge, and very little on the written law.'[27]

To discuss the legal penalities for homosexuality in

isolation is also unhistorical in as much as it leaves out of account the enormous advances made in the field of 'therapy'. Whereas in former times the criminal law was the only institutional instrument of anti-homosexual repression, so that the abolition of legal penalties could indeed be equated with a renunciation of institutional backing for the taboo on homosexuality, this is in no way the case today. Society now has a new instrument of oppression, and homosexuals face a new danger, in the highly refined techniques of behaviour therapy and brain surgery which can be used to far greater effect than legislation ever could.[28]

As a result of scientific and technical progress, therefore, even a commitment to formal legal equality between homosexuals and heterosexuals is quite compatible with support for the continuing taboo on homosexuality and the maintenance of discrimination against homosexuals. A good example of this attitude was the criticism that Tobias Brocher made of the intended legal reform of 1962. Brocher expressly set out the motives that inspired his objection to a general criminalisation: 'Support for abolition of the offence of simple homosexuality can very well go together with a concern to contain and restrict homosexuality'.[29] Brocher did not criticise the legislators for seeking to contain the spread of homosexuality, but simply for the wrong means that they used for this goal. He went on to instruct the legislature that it needed to find a relationship between end and means geared more to the findings of modern science:

It would certainly be wrong for the legislature to obstruct someone who has got into the deviation of homosexuality from openly seeking treatment for his psychosexual backwardness, due to a general defamation on the basis of inadequate understanding of the results of scientific investigation. Only a tolerance of possible wrong developments and the corrective they require can create the subjective preparedness to overcome them.[30]

Here Brocher indicates the manifold possibilities of therapy. But the only forms of therapy he can have in mind are those whose professed goal is to bring the homosexual patient to heterosexual functioning. How else could he think of containing homosexuality? The practice of such forms of therapy, however, is dependent on certain external conditions. One of the most essential prerequisites for the efficacy of any therapy to do away with homosexuality is that this is the patient's 'free decision'. Harsh anti-homosexual legislation, however, obstructs the widespread use of this other instrument, because, Brocher seems to assume, the legal defamation of homosexuals prevents or at least makes more difficult an internalisation of guilt:

Existing legislation makes it impossible to change homosexual behaviour by working through and overcoming infantile residues, which appears doubly questionable when viewed in the perspective of resocialisation that is supposed to be the aim of all criminal legislation.[31]

This resocialisation, by which Brocher evidently means the heterosexualisation of homosexuals, seems to him ruled out because the general defamation of homosexuals as criminal has the effect of externalising their inferiority and leading them to stubbornly persist in their ways, thus ultimately reinforcing the homosexual subculture. All these factors make things difficult for therapists who promise to do away with homosexuality, and drastically curtail the scope of such forms of therapy.

The broad spectrum of therapies developed in the course of shifting homosexuality from the realm of criminology to that of psychology gives Brocher and his kind their first real opportunity. Therapeutic techniques are now available, with whose aid manifest homosexuality actually can be inhibited. And in this way a homophobic society can once again dream of achieving a utopia free from homosexuals, for the first time (leaving aside the fascist mass murder) since the abolition of the death penalty for homosexual 'crimes' in the 18th century.

According to a certain model of interpretation that is popular today, the deep-rooted anti-psychological attitudes that are widespread among homosexuals are simply a response to the suffering they incur from the exposure and elucidation of those mental mechanisms that have a determining effect on their life. But this is only one factor. Another is to be sought in the theory and practice of many branches of psychology and medicine. The rejection of psychology is in part a response to its actual practice, containing a genuine fear at the threat proceeding from psychology itself and all other scientific disciplines that claim to have arisen in order to help people. This fear leads to an all-round rejection of psychology and a resort to biologistic and even racist theories of homosexuality, or at least to theories that are invariably objectivist and completely dispense with the subject.

The attraction of biologistic theories or rigid anthropological ideas, which pervade the literary and theoretical expressions of the homosexual movement, reflects the fear of an 'extinction' of homosexuality. What is feared, of course, is not the extinction of a possibility inscribed in the nature of human erotic drive as such. It is the justified fear of an extinction of homosexual individuals. This real threat is also responsible for the fact that people cannot accept the distinction between the category of homosexuals (as concrete, persecuted and oppressed individuals) and that of homosexuality (as an unliberated human drive). Because of this, it happens time and again, even in recent years of the gay liberation movement,[32] that homosexuals as they exist today are abstracted from the social context and given a biological anchorage, or else the present forms of homosexuality are given an anthropological validity.

2. Homosexuality and Anthropology

Anthropological assumptions and ideas of morality always occupy a central place in debates on homosexuality and homosexuals, just as in discussion of those sexual phenomena classified as 'perversions'. Since the sexual research of recent years has rejected any explicit engagement with anthropology and ethics, it has tended to overlook the strong hold that ethical and anthropological ideas still have. The impression is given that any notion seeking to dogmatically define the essence of sexuality as heterosexual is a thing of the past. Yet within the scientific arena this ideology has only remained silent and more or less repressed. The conviction that homosexuality is somehow incorrect still remains very often the underlying motivation for theoretical and practical concern with it. Even when a scientific investigation of sexual phenomena expressly distances itself from the anthropological and ethical ideas that provide a foundation for the norms of a particular social epoch, it cannot simply avoid their effects. Thus even a scientist like Kinsey, seeking to confine himself to presenting 'factual data on human sexual behaviour',[1] still constantly relates this to a concept of value. And where the prevailing social tendency is to stamp anything different as degenerate, then even a discussion of 'deviant' modes of sexual behaviour which is aware of this tendency finds it hard to avoid a misinterpretation of its results.

This dilemma is readily apparent in the investigations of human sexual behaviour by Kinsey and his fellow workers. On the one hand they impose on themselves a strict neutrality, yet at the same time the fictitious character of this neutrality cannot help but show through. They say, for example, in an essay on sexual perversions:

> Nothing that we previously said, or that we shall say here, should be taken to constitute any judgement on the moral acceptability or unacceptability of the so-called sexual perversions, or their desirability as a way of life in our current social organisation.[2]

The interpretation of the data produced is left to others 'who are trained to consider matters of ethics and of social values'.[3] This abdication, however, destroys the assumed neutrality. Social conditions do not permit a neutrality of this kind, and so an attitude of aloofness simply collapses into one of people who don't like to get their hands dirty.

Theories of homosexuality have a complex and changing history, and anthropological assumptions have served to justify homosexuals as well as to criticise them. It is true that research into homosexuality has generally been undertaken on the basis of anthropologcal principles that assume heterosexuality to be the only form of sexual satisfaction proper for human beings. This assumption is used deductively, and modes of sexual behaviour that depart from it are classified accordingly. Alternatively, however, homosexuality can be defined as equally valid, or at least a possible alternative, and there are those who have actually seen it as a superior form of sexuality.

What has been decisive in the former case, as far as the assessment of sexual perversions and homosexuality goes, is the age-old persecution of any sexual behaviour labelled 'deviant'. The way these forms have been dealt with in the past is given a transhistorical validity. Even the general anthropological study of sexuality, according to one of its

best-known representatives, von Gebsattel, raises the
question of the 'objective meaning' of sexual life.[4]
Anthropology investigates 'the ordering of sexual life in
terms of the overall meaning of human existence. Given
that order has to be struggled for, disorder always
threatens; departures from the objective meaning of sexual
life that is viewed as the "norm" are a matter for medical
anthropology'.[5]

The norm is thus ascribed an essentially rational
meaning, and sexual perversions accordingly condemned.
This leads to a fundamentally hostile attitude towards
modes of sexual behaviour that deviate from the posited
norm. Concealed in this conception of the norm is the
notion of a unitary basic pattern, the source of order,
which while not determining human behaviour directly,
does do so in the last instance. The historical persecution of
those who depart from the norm must accordingly be
understood as a defence of this basic pattern. The question
of the meaning of perverse sexual behaviour, and the
answers this is given, have always taken for granted the
exclusion of the sexual perversions from the acknowledged
system of norms. In this sense, anthropology with this
orientation has actually legitimised, in retrospect, the
persecution and defamation of deviant sexual behaviour.

Yet even anthropological ideas that were supportive of
homosexuality, once they came to form the basis for
systematic research, could not avoid a historical legacy
that included the persecution of homosexuals and the
anthropological legitimation of this. The verdict on
homosexuality pronounced by Christian ethics has always
been anchored in a rigid anthropology that defines
sexuality as involving the two sexes and restricts it to its
procreative function. All sexual practices that challenge
the primacy of procreation are unnatural and consequent-

ly immoral. The strength of resistance mobilised against them depends on the extent to which these 'deviant' practices vary from the postulated essence of sexuality.[6] Practices that seem no more than a substitute for the norm attract only mild condemnation. Forms of sexuality that emphasise the aspect of pleasure over that of duty, yet do not abandon duty altogether, can hope for leniency. But no mercy is shown in attacking those forms seen as exclusively oriented towards enjoyment and excess. In the condemnation of homosexuality as a phenomenon of decadence and jaded appetites, we can trace the ancient hatred with which domesticated sexuality proclaims its misguided protest.

This hierarchy of persecution can even bear on homosexuality itself. It reaches a peak in the vengeful disdain for anal intercourse. The reason this attracts so much hatred is that it is both so akin to heterosexual genital contact, yet at the same time negates the procreative function of sexuality so decisively.[7] The argument that the meaninglessness and misdirection of homosexuality is a function of the physiological characteristics of the two sexes and a sexuality corresponding to this breaks down completely when faced with anal intercourse between homosexual men. Here, just as in heterosexual contact, there is a receptive and a penetrating partner. According to recent research, the regular practice of anal intercourse leads the anus to assume the function of a receptive organ in a quite exemplary way, so that it is almost possible to speak of a 'vaginisation' of the anus. The particular form of 'indecency' practised in anal-genital contact, moreover, also demolishes what is seen as the eternal active character of the male role in sex, and this is the fundamental reason for the stubbornness with which it is slandered. Most disturbing of all, then, are those men who abandon the male definition of being the subject of sexuality, i.e. the role of aggressive penetration, and present themselves as objects by accepting anal intercourse. The logical conclusion is that men who behave in this way should no longer be recognised as such. And their betrayal of masculinity is viewed so seriously that any hope of their re-attaining the sexual role seen as biologically proper and natural must be abandoned. The prognoses for therapeutic intervention are correspondingly unfavourable.

Ferenczi, for example, deemed what he saw as the pure type of passive homosexual or 'subject homoerotic' — a man who in intercourse with men feels himself to be a woman. . .and this not only in genital intercourse, but in all relations of life' — as beyond the powers of psychoanalysis to cure.[8] The prognosis for his pure type of 'active homosexual', on the other hand, was altogether more favourable: 'The true "active homosexual". . .feels himself a man in every respect, is as a rule very energetic and active, and there is nothing effeminate to be discovered in his bodily or mental organisation.'[9] The degree to which Ferenczi was dominated by the equations active = masculine and passive = feminine is shown by an observation that today seems quite grotesque:

> It must further be remarked that many inverts are by
> no means quite insusceptible to the endearments of
> the female sex. It is through intercourse with woman
> (i.e. their like) that they dispose of what may be called
> the homosexual component of their sexuality.[10]

In Ferenczi's classification and its ensuing prognosis, the active homosexual is thus defined as a proper man simply on the grounds of his apparent behaviour. This classification, however, is based on a re-interpretation which makes the sexuality of all 'active homosexuals' into a kind of 'emergency homosexuality', their 'passive' partner being simply the substitute for an object of opposite sex. By sleight of hand, every homosexual act is reduced to pseudo-homosexuality, with the result that heterosexuality in its traditional form remains the sole and unchallenged representative of human sexuality.[11]

3. The Biologising of Ethics

The new sexual science that emerged at the end of the 19th century set out to secularise the traditional Christian ethics. What had previously been viewed as inferior simply from a moral standpoint was now to be anchored in biology. Krafft-Ebing declared as perverted 'any expression of the sexual impulse which fails to correspond to the purposes of nature, i.e. of procreation, on the assumption that normal sexual satisfaction is practicable.'[1] He classified homosexuality as a mental illness, and this was long to remain the last word in established medicine. True, this later came to shift the ground of its classification away from the rather strange arguments of Krafft-Ebing;[2] yet for a long while homosexuality remained as he had defined it: a 'functional sign of degeneracy', a 'part-manifestation of a neuropathic condition mostly determined by heredity'.[3]

This conception of homosexuality very soon came under criticism, particularly from those who felt in their own person the annihilating verdict pronounced against them; not perhaps for the first time, but now newly endowed with the dignity of science. Given the unbroken dominance of anthropological and teleological notions in the sexual research of this time, critics of the sickness theory were compelled to back up their own arguments in a similar fashion. Contrary evidence had to be brought forward, if the painful history of homosexuals was finally to take a turn for the better. The attempt was therefore made to replace the old anthropology, in which homosexuals appeared only as sick and severely disabled, by a new anthropology whose categories enabled homosexuality to be interpreted as a sexual phenomenon compatible with the purposes of nature. As Ivan Bloch put it, writing as a homosexual representative, once it was understood that homosexuality was a 'primary natural condition. . ., the former conception of what was right would be replaced by a new one which would imperiously demand the abolition of legislation that persecutes and libels a natural phenomenon as a disability'.[4]

4. An Alternative Anthropology

Magnus Hirschfeld was one of the sharpest critics of the idea that homosexuality was in any way pathological. While also championing the view that it was biologically rooted, Hirschfeld linked this together with ideas developed several decades previously by K. H. Ulrichs, in various 'anthropological studies on sexual love between men'.[1] Ulrichs' very first publication already contains the central tenets of his theory of a 'healthy homosexuality', which he was later to refine step by step in further works. According to Ulrichs, one of the first fighters for homosexual emancipation,[2] homosexuality was an inborn natural disposition, a physiological phenomenon but in no way pathological:

> There is a class of born Urnings [=Uranians], a class of individuals who are born with the sexual drive of women and have male bodies. They are a subspecies of men whose Uranian love is congenital...By congenital is meant sexual, organic and mental inheritance, not an inherited disease and not such inheritances as pyromania, kleptomania and alcoholism, but rather an inheritance such as Dionians [=normal men] receive in their sexual drives towards women and vice versa.[3]

Since Ulrichs saw homosexuals as born that way, it followed that they could not act unnaturally, but acted quite 'naturally' in terms of their particular drives.

How progressive Ulrichs was in his time can be seen

from his criticism of the then prevailing view that the essence of sexuality was to serve procreation. As against this reduction, he emphasised the aspect of sexual pleasure, seeing this as a no less essential part of sexuality. Nor did he seek to apply this expanded conception only to homosexuality; it was to cover heterosexual relations as well. Ulrichs also seems to have been convinced of the existence of certain surplus sexual needs in heterosexual men which they could not satisfy with women, writing: 'Nature did not create Dionians for women alone, but also for Uranians. . .to fulfil the need of a non-productive, sexual, natural activity.'[4] The homosexual thus served as a kind of stand-in for the satisfaction of all those sexual desires of heterosexual men that could not be met by women.

The root of this peculiar turn in Ulrichs' theory lies in his enthusiasm for virility. Just like Blüher,[5] hymning inter-male eroticism at a later date, Ulrichs was a champion of masculine supremacy, though from a rather different angle. For Blüher, the object was to rebut the 'feminine' features of homosexual men that Hirschfeld and Ulrichs had stressed, or at least not repudiated, and to emphasise the masculine element in homosexuality. The ideas of Ulrichs revolve around masculinity in a different way, but fall prey to it all the same:

> If we [Uranians] were not feminine men by nature, but rather, as you [Dionians] maintain, true men who voluntarily divert: then girlish young men would supposedly be more attractive to us than masculine ones. However, just as women, we are attracted only by truly masculine young men. Unmanly ones leave us cold.[6]

For the same reasons, Ulrichs equally ruled out the

possibility of sexual attraction between homosexual men; for here too the most important precondition of 'true masculinity'[7] was lacking.

This allegiance to virility, the avowed desire for union with an unchallenged masculinity, simply expresses the lack of masculinity felt in oneself, which identification with a partner of the same sex is intended to strengthen. If the lack of masculinity is very pronounced — and this is a function of both the relative social deprecation of homosexuals and the social glorification of the masculine — then the heterosexual man is far more suitable a partner for this identificatory borrowing of masculinity. He alone can provide complete satisfaction, for he alone, according to the prevailing ideas, fully merits the label of man.

Ulrichs was certainly quite aware that by this biologising of homosexuality he gave homosexuals the fate of an eternal minority. His theoretical discussions are pervaded by the attempt to procure for this 'natural' social minority a secure and appropriate place in society. This was the function of his anthropological scheme, with its system of categories permitting the integration of male homosexuality. The old anthropological doctrine of constants was shattered, yet only to expand it by a new constant. Ulrichs did not manage to advance to a more open anthropological position, which could also account for other groups departing from the present social norm. By remaining trapped in teleology, his model ultimately led to an insuperable contradiction. While the anthropology he criticised maintained that nature produced only men and women, and a sexuality corresponding to this, he held that nature had also produced a third variant, homosexuals, these being equally in harmony with posited natural purposes.[8]

The personality of the investigator is more clearly

present in Ulrichs' writings than in those of his successors, even when these were also homosexual themselves. This makes them instructive to read still today, in a sense that goes beyond the ideas they directly contain. Ulrichs' subjective involvement also comes through in a characteristic and exaggerated justification for homosexuals, at points inflated to elitist claims. The monstrous oppression of homosexuals as unnatural, morally despicable and biologically inferior is countered by a superior system of homosexuality. This can sometimes go so far as to make homosexuality the pillar of a more rational social order.[9] The compulsive search for justification, however, only expresses the threatened existence of the homosexual subject. It is this, and not any firm feeling of superiority, that is the basic reason for the elitist boasting which especially marks biologically oriented research on homosexuality, and is reflected in its supporters as the belief that they belong to a special kind of people, ascribed by nature certain special social tasks. This elitism results from the collective inferiority feelings of homosexuals, a fragment of these finding its way into the research process itself.

The attraction to biology also expresses a certain unconscious fear of destruction on the part of the individual homosexual researcher. The attempt is made, with great pains, to produce for the inhuman and anti-homosexual society evidence that will disprove all its paranoid ideas. But since rational objections seem in vain against the power of irrationality, and the painful experience of homosexuals makes its own contribution to a pessimistic view of history, history is completely exculpated and homosexuals made entirely into a fact of nature.

If Hirschfeld's discussions of homosexual liberation

An Alternative Anthropology

sound a less optimistic note than those of Ulrichs, this is attributable to the change in historical circumstances. Ulrichs wrote at a time when the demands of Christian morality had been partly beaten back, and had not yet been completely re-secularised. The liberation of the individual in the bourgeois revolution, together with the ideas of the Enlightenment, had also led to a liberal view on homosexuality. By Ulrichs' time, not all German states still followed the pulpit in their legislation and there was a clear tendency towards decriminalisation.

This process began in France, where from 1810 onwards so-called pederasty was no longer deemed a crime. The Bavarian legislation of 1813 was the first in Germany to follow the Code Napoléon; it was drafted by A. von Feuerbach, the founder of the modern German criminal code. Feuerbach's *Manual of Generally Prevailing German Criminal Law* appeared in new editions throughout the 19th century, achieving a broad circulation for his liberal views. Since Feuerbach saw the essence of crime as lying only in damage to private or state rights, he was able to remove homosexuality from the statute book. According to the new Bavarian legislation, 'so long as indecent activities only infringe on morality, without injuring any other right, this law does not apply'.[10]

During the 1840s, the states of Brunswick, Hanover and Baden essentially adopted this liberal standpoint, and passed legislation that no longer penalised 'simple' homosexuality. Prussia, on the other hand, maintained the criminal sanction. After the founding of the Reich in 1871, paragraph 143 of the old Prussian legislation was taken over as paragraph 175 of the new Reich penal code. As far as homosexuals were concerned, the Enlightenment was at an end, and with it the hope that all German states would gradually adopt the views of Feuerbach.[11]

Under the new and more repressive historical circumstances which Hirschfeld faced, it seemed sensible on practical grounds alone to give homosexuals a natural basis, i.e. a biological guarantee. Guided by the same practical considerations as Ulrichs had been before, Hirschfeld developed a theory in which homosexuals formed an innate intermediate type between man and woman, and should be considered a 'third sex'.[12] Hirschfeld battled untiringly to spread his theory, deeply convinced that its general acceptance was the *sine qua non* for the social recognition of homosexuals.

5. Hirschfeld's Debate with Psychoanalysis

Hirschfeld's position was not only diametrically opposed to the sickness theory prevalent in sexual research and psychiatry; he equally distanced himself from those theories that attributed homosexuality to external and contingent factors. With the development of psychoanalysis, however, Hirschfeld's conception found a new critic. The psychoanalytic theory of the infantile origins of manifest homosexuality stood in sharp contradiction to Hirschfeld's view, and he eventually had to oppose it in the most drastic terms. Till the end of his life, Hirschfeld was unable to accept the psychoanalytic standpoint. This is somewhat remarkable, in that Freud in his *Three Essays on Sexuality* did not dispense with a natural basis for homosexuality, but in fact pronounced homosexuality a general human disposition and demonstrated that 'libidinal attachments to persons of the same sex play no less a part as factors in normal mental life . . . than do similar attachments to the opposite sex'.[1]

In one of his last works, *The Science of Sex*, Hirschfeld summarised once again his objections to psychoanalysis, and came to the following conclusion:

I have sincerely tried to fathom the views put forward in recent years by Freud and his school, designed to show the influence of non-constitutional factors. But the more I have done so, the more clearly I have found that what Freud's doctrine maintains as to the effect of external childhood events on human sexual development is fundamentally incorrect.[2]

How unsuccessful were Hirschfeld's efforts to understand psychoanalysis is shown by the '12 key points'[3] he presents in this book, leading to 'the inescapable conclusion that homosexuality involves a "deep-seated constitutional" disposition'.[4] Leaving aside biological characteristics or statistical results that lie outside the field of psychoanalysis, all Hirschfeld's other points are perfectly compatible with the psychoanalytic doctrine of the infantile genesis of manifest homosexuality.

There is still the question as to why Hirschfeld could not understand the theory of psychoanalysis and integrate it into his own viewpoint, why he could rest content with the 'crude explanation that everyone is born with his sexual instinct attached to a particular sexual object'.[5] One of the more superficial reasons for Hirschfeld's insistence that homosexuality was an innate intermediate type may be sought in simple tactical considerations. The 'Scientific Humanitarian Committee' that he founded was locked in struggle for the abolition of paragraph 175. In the debate on the 'criminality' of homosexuality at the time, Hirschfeld's theory played a prominent role. And as the public prosecutor Ludwig Ebermayer typically maintained in the *German Medical Weekly* in 1924, the decision whether to repeal the law against homosexuality was seen as dependent on whether homosexuals were compelled by their biology to a same-sex choice of partner:

> If homosexual intercourse, as a general rule, is simply the expression of a deep-seated constitutional disposition, then the state scarcely has any cause to make this a punishable offence. Assuming the above assumption to be correct, then the essential

determinant of criminality, i.e. guilt, would be lacking, for someone who acts simply as an expression of a deep-seated constitutional disposition does not act in a blameworthy way. He does not will to go against the law, and only someone who acts in a blameworthy way can properly be penalised.[6]

In this kind of position, and the exculpation it promised, Hirschfeld evidently saw the fruits of his entire theoretical and practical work. He expressly agreed that the criminality of homosexuals 'should be above all a question of their "deep-seated constitutional disposition". This has been my aim in the battle I have waged throughout my life on behalf of those deprived of their rights'.[7]

Even when we take into account that Hirschfeld saw public acceptance of his theory, i.e. its utilitarian aspect, as evidence for its truth, and similarly as evidence for the falsity of the psychoanalytic standpoint, his apologetic commentary on this legalistic quotation is still somewhat surprising. The public prosecutor's reference to a 'deep-seated constitutional disposition' is simply another expression for an innate mental degeneration, involving not only a compulsion to homosexuality, but also — and this is the decisive step in the argument — a somewhat distorted interpretation of reality. The decriminalisation to which Hirschfeld looked forward, in other words, meant a partial immunity from prosecution on grounds of irresponsibility. If this were true, then that alone would be sufficient reason for revising paragraph 175, for it is senseless to keep in force a law that cannot be properly applied since the offending party is unable to understand the guilt of his actions. In the legal sense, however, homosexuals certainly do act in a 'guilty' way. Every homosexual in Germany as elsewhere was certainly well aware of going against the law if he had homosexual contacts. Whether he considered the law right or wrong was a different matter, as also whether he felt guilty in any sense other than the criminal one. In no case is there any plausible reason for assuming that homosexuals as such 'do not have the same sovereignty and degree of freedom in relation to their sexuality'[8] as do heterosexuals. Removal of the principle of criminal responsibility in the case of 'homosexual offences' would deprive homosexuals of a fundamental dimension of their existence, i.e. their normality in the psychiatric sense of the term.

It is difficult to imagine the effects an immunity granted on grounds such as these would have had on the general consciousness of homosexuals. At its core, Ebermayer's line of argument gives fuel to the prejudice that is unwilling to trust homosexuals not only in the field of sexuality, but in the wider field of social life as well. Legal immunity granted at the price of separation into a biological category would not only leave the moral verdict unaffected, but would keep it in its biologised form. The question posed here is not whether the concept of guilt should be used in connection with homosexuality at all, but simply whether the guilty party acts from a 'deep-seated compulsion', and this leaves quite untouched the key social idea that makes homosexuality guilty in the first place, i.e. the heterosexual demand for hegemony.

How little the argument of an innate and thus 'natural' homosexuality managed to achieve in a society concerned to protect a form of sexuality appearing to correspond to its particular principles and requirements, is shown by the reasons given in the draft penal code of 1962. In this document, the idea that homosexuality involves a 'natural' and thus unobjectionable drive is declared irrelevant for legislation: 'If the viewpoint underlying this assumption were accepted, society would have to accept and honour every variety of human nature as natural, no matter how degenerate.'[9]

It must at least be conceded that this shows a more accurate conception of human sexuality than is expressed in the view that ties homosexuality to biology. Human sexuality and its forms of expression are not ready-made things, but a complex of processes that is mediated through the human interaction with nature, i.e. ultimately through work. Human needs certainly do have a natural basis, but 'there are no natural human needs, this expression is inherently contradictory'.[10]

6. The Reduction of Homosexuality to the Homosexual

If the concern of Hirschfeld and the biologistic theory of homosexuality in general had simply been to show evidence of a natural basis for homosexuality, this would not have come into such diametrical opposition to psychoanalysis as it necessarily did. The object of Hirschfeld's research, however, was to anchor homosexuals as a particular human sub-species. And this he managed to do only by an obstinate reduction of homosexuality to the manifest homosexual.

The findings of psychoanalysis show a way of avoiding this traditional reduction, as well as providing a socio-psychological explanation for the hatred of homosexuals.[1] In the light of psychoanalysis, Hirschfeld's standpoint can be seen as far too restricted. Being unable to distinguish between the categories 'homosexual' and 'homosexuality', he had to see the essence and appearance of homosexuality as identical. In this way, however, advance in knowledge was sacrificed to mere accumulation of data, and Hirschfeld's own writings are impoverished in this respect.

The categories 'homosexuality' and 'homosexual' need in fact to be clearly distinguished. They represent two different levels or fields, and while not in contradiction, they are far indeed from being one and the same. There is a discrepancy between homosexuality as a possibility that is part and parcel of the human endowment, and homosexuality as this is found in manifest homosexuals — a discrepancy that can only be resolved in practice. The aim of this resolution is not simply a democratic reconciliation between a majority (heterosexuals) and a minority (homosexuals). It has rather a utopian dimension, being led by the aspiration of attaining social relations in which the collective repression of the homosexual component can be liberated, thus making superfluous the questionable sublimations and reaction-formations this involves. So long as homosexuality appears only in a compulsive form, and can in a sense be practised only as an 'emergency solution', empirical investigation of homosexual individuals cannot yield sufficient evidence as to the nature of homosexuality itself.

Once the separation between the two categories is conceded, each representing a different zone of the homosexual taboo, i.e. the category 'homosexual' more strongly its social (conscious) side and the category 'homosexuality' more strongly its mental (unconscious) side, then it is easier to avoid the danger of seeing the form of homosexuality apparent in manifest homosexuals as the ultimate source of evidence. An empirical investigation of homosexuals cannot seek to come to grips with homosexuality as such, but only with homosexuality in its particular, socially imposed form, as displayed by the life of homosexual individuals in a particular social epoch.

Thus despite his constant protestations to the contrary, the actual object of Hirschfeld's research was never homosexuality. His interest bore rather on the particular phenomenon displayed by the homosexual individuals of his time. This is particularly striking with regard to the '12 points' he adduced as proof of the innate character of the homosexual object-choice.[2]

7. Psychoanalysis versus Sexology

The most important objections to Hirschfeld and his followers from the psychoanalytic standpoint were formulated by Freud himself. Without mentioning Hirschfeld's name directly, Freud took issue with him on several occasions.[1] Among these is the celebrated note added to the *Three Essays on Sexuality* in 1915, which should be read as a direct answer to Hirschfeld:

Psychoanalytic research is most decidedly opposed to any attempt at separating off homosexuals from the rest of mankind as a group of a special character. By studying sexual excitations other than those that are manifestly displayed, it has found that all human beings are capable of making a homosexual object-choice and have in fact made one in their unconscious . . . On the contrary, psychoanalysis considers that a choice of an object independently of its sex — freedom to range equally over male and female objects — as it is found in childhood, in primitive states of society and early periods of history, is the original basis from which, as a result of restriction in one direction or the other, both the normal and the inverted types develop. Thus from the point of view of psychoanalysis the exclusive sexual interest felt by men for women is also a problem that needs elucidating and is not a self-evident fact based upon an attraction that is ultimately of a chemical nature.[2]

What is most striking here is less Freud's specific

theoretical conception than the difference in social practice his remarks imply.

For that branch of etiological research whose main interest lies in biology, the problem comes to an end once it is established that homosexuals are an intermediate sexual type. A social practice with this orientation reaches its goal once homosexuals are recognised as a group of a special character, this recognition to be attained 'by educating the population as to the nature of homosexuality'.[3] The theoretical objectives and practical solutions that follow from the Freudian challenge are far less simple. What is now required is a complete theoretical explanation of the mental and social mechanisms that bring about the results of homosexuality and heterosexuality. This would overthrow the whole etiological procedure, including that used by psychoanalysis itself, since this has still not ceased attempting to explain 'deviance' as an isolated phenomenon. Freud's demand that compulsory heterosexuality should also be investigated, the field being widened to embrace the sexual development of all human beings, has thus still to be met. In this respect, psychoanalysis has not yet measured up to its own claims. If it sees homosexuality as a category of human sexuality, and not just a category to be applied to homosexuals, it should turn its attention to repressed homosexuality, the mechanisms of repression and the return of the repressed at least as intensively as it studies the manifest appearance of homosexuality in the shape of homosexual individuals.

The Freudian model is not based on closed anthropological assumptions, and a social practice with this inspiration cannot be content simply to bring about the social acceptance of homosexuals. The 'restriction in one direction or the other' which Freud mentioned has its roots in the demands of culture, and not in supposedly innate natural goals. The types that arise as the result of this restriction, oriented either to the same or the opposite sex, are formed by social forces, and hence the solution can only be a social one, not just individual. Neither form of object-choice is dictated by a special sexual drive, no matter what this might be, but both are rather the result of individual experience and historical process.

Freud persistently held fast to the common mental structure of homosexuals and heterosexuals, and was not led astray even by such differences as may well exist. Where such differences are present, even when they involve more than the most external forms of behaviour and bear on the whole development of the personality, they still do not point to any qualitative difference in the circumstances that lead to a homosexual object-choice. On this point Freud noted: 'The difference in the end-products may be of a qualitative nature, but analysis shows that the differences between their determinants are only quantitative'.[4] These 'differences in the end-products' involve certain secondary phenomena that can be completely attributed to social conditions. They in no way point to a self-sufficient homosexual nature.[5]

We saw above the reasons that prevented Hirschfeld from understanding the essential theories of psychoanalysis vis-à-vis homosexuality, these reasons basically involving practical considerations. But a further factor might well have been anxiety as to the implications of psychoanalytic theory for himself. For whether intentionally so or not, as far as homosexuals were concerned psychoanalytic theory and practice were part and parcel of medical efforts aiming to combat the 'evil' in homosexual individuals. These efforts were spelled out, in relation to psychiatric and sexological thinking, by A. von Eulenburg in his Preface to I. Bloch's *Contributions to the Etiology of Psychopathia Sexualis*:

The doctrine of the 'innate' character of sexual perversions, and homosexuality in particular, must therefore be abandoned or at least considerably restricted. We doctors are certainly the last people to shed a tear over it; for if the evils we are dealing with are acquired, and moreover in most cases acquired as a result of external and contingent factors, or else artificially induced, then we shall feel in a far better position than before to intervene effectively against them, both with a view to curing them, and above all to preventing them by prophylactic means.[6]

It should be clear enough that this argument cannot be put forward in quite the same way on the basis of a psychoanalytic theory of the genesis of homosexuality. The distrust that homosexuals feel towards psychoanalysis, which is still not overcome today, is also fuelled by an erroneous equation of the psychoanalytic conception with the ideas of psychiatry. But this is also perpetuated by the psychoanalytic tradition itself, as shown recently in the case of Socarides,[7] the latest exponent of a tradition that is unwilling to oppose the social repression of homosexuals.

8. Anthropological Psychiatry

Hirschfeld's dogmatic biological anthropology had little success in the German medical establishment. The ideas that came to prevail here were based above all on so-called 'anthropological psychiatry', linked with the names of O. Schwarz, E. Strauss, H. Kunz and V.E. von Gebsattel. The theoretical interest of this variant of perversion research, which can in a certain sense be described as an 'ethical anthropology',[1] bore less on organic peculiarities than on their social and mental accompaniments, and on showing the abnormal character of these. Of central importance in this conception were the concepts of 'deformation' and 'mania'. 'Deformation', as defined by Strauss, was to express the fact that 'we do not see self-destruction and the destruction of institutions and achievements as the external result of manias and perversions, but rather hold self-destruction and the destruction of social norms to be their hidden significance'.[2] 'Mania', for its part, was understood as a dynamic inherent to the perversions, bringing an incessant increase in sexual excitation without offering any possibility of satisfaction.

Tracing the historical development of the concept of 'sexual mania', E. Schorsch came to the conclusion: 'Only when so-called anthropological psychiatry . . . came to subsume the perversions expressly under an expanded concept of mania was perversion described as a progressively abnormal development of the personality'.[3]

Anthropological psychiatry ascribed the perversions a

basically different significance from anything before. Viewed simply as a sign of sickness and degeneration, the phenomenon was purely individual in scope. Sickness causes suffering primarily to the patient afflicted by it, and to a certain extent those around him. When perversion was seen as a sickness, there was no immediate danger to the constitution of society as a whole. But if the hidden significance of perversions was that of destroying social norms, they became a threat of immense proportions, which could not just be fought by medicine alone, this necessarily continuing to view the individual affected as a patient.[4] It was now the task of all social institutions to concern themselves with perversion, at least all those with a stake in preserving the basic essence of the 'various interpersonal relations and the norms they embody'.[5] This task arose on the one hand from the precarious status of these norms, which were 'constantly threatened and often damaged by disturbing hostile factors', this having something to do with the 'character of social conditions'[6], while on the other hand it arose from the definition of the perversions as precisely one of those elements that threaten the objectively valid norm.

There is a striking analogy between the underlying anthropological position here and that put forward a few years later by Arnold Gehlen in his book *Mankind* (1st edition 1940).[7] Indeed, ideas that were still fragmentary and little systematised in anthropological psychiatry can only be fully understood from the perspective of the anthropological system developed by Gehlen.

Gehlen conceived human beings as governed by instincts, submerged by their drives and at extreme risk — an endangered species. As such, they need rigid social institutions and norms. Caught up in these institutions, they are freed from their burdens to the extent that both individual life and the survival of the species are guaranteed.[8] In order to take any part in society and contribute to its continuance, they must not only surrender themselves to the force of institutions; they must work actively to keep these stable. As Schelsky[9] expressed it, only those who accept 'the alienation of their impulses into the institutions' and 'renounce the subjectivity of their drives and constitution'[10] have any claim to be defined as full members of society. The institutions and norms handed down by tradition were seen not only as historically necessary, but as fundamentally correct and rational; they claimed a transhistorical validity. Those whose sexual impulses have not been domesticated are thus antisocial, and actually dangerous in the sense of a higher reason. Schelsky continues:

> Behaviour in accordance with the norm, i.e. morality, has no intrinsic value unless it makes possible these higher forms of human existence, both for the individual and for society . . . Those who depart from the norm are not condemned to a marginal role just by an arbitrary social standard, acting merely in public opinion and social consciousness; the verdict of the norm is the assertion by a culture that these groups are incapable of attaining the higher forms of individual or social existence that this culture supports.[11]

It is clear from such formulations that the sociological direction taken by the norm in Schelsky's writings in no way meant any relaxation of Gehlen's dogmatic anthropological conception. In both cases the intention was the same, i. e. rigorous defence against perversion, so that it ultimately doesn't matter whether the norms that define proper sexual behaviour have no historical reference-point whatsoever, or whether they are seen as determined by culture. In Schelsky's *Sociology of Sexuality*, where the verdict of anthropological failure and deformation is supplemented by one of failure to meet higher cultural forms of existence, rejection of the perversions comes to assume a truly totalitarian character. The lower forms of existence where perversions of all kinds are to be found do not involve a mere non-attainment of the higher levels of culture, in the sense of backwardness; perversion is seen as a permanent rebellion against fundamentally rational cultural achievements. The social invalidity of the perversions, which is still maintained, no longer lies simply in their 'lack of biological purpose'. It is now described as an essentially destructive and antisocial element. Indulgence or toleration of sexual perversions, let alone approval, bears the danger of a decay into barbarism:

> With the rise and differentiation of institutionalised levels of personal and social existence and behaviour, the rigour of morality grows as well, with a more acute moral exclusion of those incapable of these forms of existence, whereas tolerance towards the abnormal and a softening of moral boundaries go together with the deterioration and decay of personal and social potentialities.[12]

The fear of perversions seems particularly great because their rebellion is directed against a central social institution, the family.[13] The family has undertaken the task of trapping human drives, changing their form and adapting them to society. In the view of conservative anthropology, the family is an essential social institution, being indispensable to the continuance of civilisation. This anthropology is therefore particularly hostile to those perversions which generally involve a refusal to found a new family. Acceptance of these perversions, for anthropology of this kind, is equivalent to a murderous assault on the status quo.

I have already mentioned how this conservative anthropology needed not the faintest glimmer of a moral doctrine in order to condemn homosexuals for immoral behaviour. In its line of thought, immoral fundamentally means those who fail to meet their cultural obligation in one important respect, and do not subject themselves to prevailing social institutions. Of course, this renunciation of morality only goes so far; a moral judgement is still made to establish the supposed antisocial character of the behaviour in question. For conservative anthropology, then, the perversions all serve a double purpose. On the one hand segments of individual behaviour are arbitrarily extracted, exaggerated and used to illustrate the results of failure to meet the demands of the present level of civilisation; on the other hand the perversions themselves are characterised as the agent of a threatening regression. Yet the perversions are little more than a paradigm here. They exemplify the basic tendency of conservative anthropology, i.e. how it seeks to put up a barrier to necessary social change by appeal to human nature.[14]

9. The Wave of Liberalism

The social and legal persecution of homosexuals, and the more or less open attempts to repress or do away with them, mean that the consciousness of homosexuals is initially formed by the prevailing consciousness about them. This is why any theory of homosexuality has a decisive bearing on the self-esteem and self-interpretation of homosexuals. What is commonly understood by homosexual self-consciousness is simply a medley of rebuttals to the prevailing anti-homosexual ideas, which may be more or less virulent. Even in its most developed form, as shown in the case of Ulrichs and Hirschfeld, homosexual ideology is no more than the negative of the general ideologies about homosexuals. But so long as social persecution continues, and new attempts are constantly made to justify it, the consciousness of homosexuals will not come into its own. It remains a consciousness of defence and justification. Always concerned to refute what is supposedly immoral or antisocial in their behaviour, homosexuals develop an acute idea of what they are not, or what they should not be, both in their own eyes and in the eyes of public opinion. As for what they are, or even how they actually behave, they have either a very incomplete idea, or indeed no idea at all.

Since anti-homosexual ideologies all seize upon arbitrarily selected aspects of homosexual behaviour in order to prove the inferior and antisocial character of homosexuality, the attempt has been made to deny differences in behaviour that are actually present and thus extinguish these from social consciousness. Homosexuals responded to the total condemnation of anthropology and the trauma they experienced under fascism with an intensified adaptation to customary ideas of normality. They were powerfully supported in these efforts by liberal sexual research, which was seeking a theoretical understanding of the homosexual phenomenon. Without any real change in essentials, this liberal sexology made homosexuals apparently equal. What was specific to homosexual existence was gradually dissolved. As a result of this process, a new mystification of homosexual experience came into being, even if this time a mystification with certain positive signs to it.[1]

While the theory of an 'intermediate sex' had a far easier way of validating the dimension of otherness,[2] as it saw this as the expression of a constitutional difference and did not have to cope with the trauma of fascism, the sexual research of the post-War era, with its positive attitude towards homosexuals, sought to emancipate them from the odium that this perceived otherness involved. Giese's *The Homosexual Man in the World* is typical in this respect. It should be seen as a cautious attempt to free homosexuals from the burden that conservative anthropology had imposed on them. Though itself having roots in the tradition of anthropological psychiatry, whose definitions of the nature and meaning of sexuality and love Giese basically shared, he wanted to remove the condemnatory label of perversion and give homosexuals back the morality that had been refused them.

Giese sought to do this by an empirical study of homosexuals,[3] the object of which was to support the conclusion he had reached in clinical practice that the behaviour of homosexuals was compatible with 'love in its normal form'. Anthropological psychiatry had seen the essence of perversion as lying in the 'absence of love in its normal form'[4], and in manic behaviour involving destruction and negation, the 'elimination, indeed the burial, of what constitutes the order and specific meaning of love and sexual life'.[5] Giese therefore sought to demonstrate forms of homosexual behaviour that were compatible with 'love in its normal form', which was no easy task in view of the homosexual behaviour he actually catalogued. But Giese could not refute the verdict of perversion simply by showing a small minority in whom the deforming and destructive aspect seemed lacking. This route had already been barred by Kunz, who had interpreted the evidence of deep tenderness in homosexual relationships as 'in general . . . phenomena of over-compensation which serve to master destruction and anxiety'.[6] What was still ultimately decisive in judging homosexuals, despite all protestations to the contrary, was the simple fact that they had rejected social constraint and had not attained heterosexuality, rather than their own particular forms of intercourse. Giese was therefore doomed to failure in his attempt to subsume at least a minority under the categories of an anthropology whose absolute and abstract claim to validity was only imposed on inferior and antisocial members of society.[7]

No matter how similar it might be to 'love in its normal form', i.e. no matter how much it might adapt to the cultural ideal, even that portion of homosexual behaviour closest to this still presents a fundamental 'deviance'. The fact that some homosexuals might behave in so 'moral' a way that their relationships cannot be distinguished from the heterosexual model does not add the slightest bit of respectability to a form of sexuality that is 'immoral' or antisocial by very definition.

Giese's investigation thus vacillated between moral

condemnation of homosexuals and their protection against the prevailing sexual morality. Its ambivalent character faithfully reflects that characteristically ambivalent tolerance which Giese typically displayed. This can be seen in the very way he deals with the empirical material, which is organised not just in terms of Giese's key anthropological categories, but also by the social climate of the time. In Giese's work we can see once again the dilemma faced even by empirical research into homosexuality from a liberal standpoint, and in a situation when the taboo seems at least somewhat more relaxed. An unreserved depiction of things that are still tabooed threatens to activate a virulent hatred, no matter what interpretation the facts are given, and in this way it can slow down or even set back the process of integration it proposes.[8] On the other hand, however, a deliberate refusal to investigate and depict homosexual reality in a comprehensive way, perhaps justified by a reference to the historical conjuncture, helps to reproduce the taboo itself. For the only way the taboo can be disturbed is by bringing to the surface things that the taboo's very purpose is to keep at a distance. If this process brings to light phenomena that inspire unease and hatred when they are first confronted, this very reaction is an argument, and not the worst one either, for an open empirical disclosure of the forbidden. An investigation of this kind, of course, merely shows the occasion for this hatred, not its underlying cause. Yet it is only possible to trace this cause and block its sources when it is accepted as a fact still to be overcome, rather than painfully trying to avoid giving the occasion for it to erupt.

Tolerance cannot be the goal of an analysis of homosexual reality conducted by and for homosexuals themselves, an analysis that does not overlook its darker sides. For tolerance becomes repressive when it seeks to reduce the behaviour and desires of real individuals to the form of love and sexuality that the present sexual morality requires. For this reason, a tactical orientation to the gradual maturing of tolerance can collapse all too easily into an intolerance towards real homosexual individuals, as its final result is to incriminate those aspects that are silently glossed over and omitted for tactical reasons. Those studies that seek to avoid phenomena which might be seen by a hypostatised sexual morality as showing homosexuals in a bad light may well claim they are protecting homosexuals from prejudice. Up to now, however, they have only given grist to a much more ominous prejudice, according to which 'the sole distinction between heterosexuals and homosexuals is that the former are attracted to the opposite sex, while the latter are attracted to the same sex'.[9] This assertion remains quite external to homosexuals, it even drives them into a new inferiority, as they can themselves perceive the very real differences that there are between them and heterosexuals, and between their morality and heterosexual morality. Though it is today so widespread and favoured, it can only be supported by a stubborn refusal to face those social constraints of which the different behaviour of homosexuals is a necessary result.

Tolerance cannot be simply an abstract principle, and this kind of statement ultimately bars the way to any tolerance that really deserves the name. What distinguishes genuine tolerance from sham tolerance is precisely its recognition of difference, and its acceptance of those who are different on their own terms. When the very real differences[10] between homosexuals and heterosexuals are ignored and flattened, then those who go against the prevailing moral ideas are given only a sham protection. In reality, this position remains completely in thrall to the totalitarian claims of the heterosexual norm, and ends up actually defending a dogmatic sexual morality against homosexuals and their forms of sexuality.

10. The Popular 'Attitude' to Homosexuals

The slogans of tolerance, decriminalisation and integration indicate a social tendency towards a breakdown of the taboo on homosexuality. Is the present tendency for tolerance more than a partial liberalisation? And should integration be taken as anything more than the subsumption of attitudes and modes of behaviour that are traditionally more widespread among homosexuals to the interest of capitalist profit?[1] Opinion polls designed to investigate the popular attitude to homosexuals have appeared to confirm the expectation that the wave of liberalisation means a significant step towards the acceptance of homosexuals. A survey by a Düsseldorf institute in 1974 provided the following classification of 'three basic attitudes towards people with a homosexual orientation':[2]

a) rejection	19.6%
b) tolerance	40.3%
c) acceptance	40.1%

This is not the place for a detailed critique of the methodology of such surveys, or a discussion of the sense, if any, in which categories such as tolerance or acceptance can be operationalised in this way. Both categories refer to emotions, and it is clear enough that direct questions of this kind cannot yield sufficient insight into the emotional disposition of the population. The emotions grasped in these categories only show themselves in any living way in social interaction between the tolerators or acceptors and the tolerated or accepted. The processes involved in such interaction, moreover, are dependent on the extent to which those involved have in fact interacted. Anyone with a modicum of mental stability might manage to accept or tolerate some random homosexual they happened to run into. It is quite different, however, when the homosexual in question is their son, daughter, husband, wife or friend. Then again, tolerance is easier said than done. An opinion survey is therefore quite unsuited for examining what is a complex network of factors.

The intention of those who commissioned this survey is evident enough from the way individual responses are classified into the three basic attitudes given. For example, all those who agreed with the statement: 'I believe homosexuals are the victims of serious prejudices which enlightened people shouldn't have' are classified as 'tolerant'. Those who held: 'The basic difference between homosexuals and other people is only in their sexual behaviour' were assigned a basic attitude of 'acceptance'. We can only assume from this crude and slapdash classification that the goal of the survey was to establish a high proportion of tolerant and accepting citizens, and in this way use the wide publicity gained to achieve a double effect.

Firstly, to make homosexuals believe they are tolerated or accepted by an increasing number of citizens. The underlying assumption seems to be that this would help to break down those subjective barriers which prevent homosexuals from claiming the 'freedoms' they are granted at the formal level. This assumption certainly has an element of truth in that a large proportion of homosexuals do view anti-homosexual aggression as more violent as this actually is. Yet it is highly dubious whether a newspaper article saying that more than 80% of the population tolerate or accept homosexuals is a suitable way of breaking down these subjective barriers that constrict their behaviour. Emotions do not follow a simple cost-benefit account, and no homosexual who is the victim of irrational fears could be induced by such an article to experiment on the premise that 'if 80% of the population now tolerate you, you can be quite open about your homosexuality, as you don't have to worry that anyone is going to react with overt aggression.' Thus even if the degree of tolerance really were as this survey indicates, it would still not be possible for those homosexuals who see things in an exaggerated way to act in a manner more fitted to the real situation. Whatever the reasons for the neurotic way they deal with the world, these are certainly not to be sought in a lack of familiarity with statistical data.

Secondly, it would seem the people who commissioned this survey hoped that the results (published in the press under headlines such as 'Homosexuals No Longer Outsiders', '40% of the Population Accept Homosexuals', etc.[3]) would have a sufficiently strong impact on those who were undecided that these too would join in the general tendency of tolerance towards homosexuals. This kind of effect, however, is no more than momentary. Just as a considerable section of the population view their traditional style of child-rearing somewhat differently after anti-authoritarian child-rearing has been propagated in the mass media — even classing it as anti-authoritarian, as they don't like to seem old-fashioned — so if there were a similar propaganda on behalf of homosexuals, many people would be more reticent about expressing their rejection. It is quite conceivable, then, that the same emotions they previously expressed as rejection would be conveyed to the next opinion pollster as tolerance.

Rather than any tolerance or acceptance of homosexuals that can be taken seriously, this opinion survey and its apparently impressive results reflect an increasing inability to accept those who are different on their own terms. In any case, there are few signs indeed that the faculties which the concept of tolerance once denoted have really become more widespread. Yet if those who fail to conform are still a problem to deal with, while at the same time the demand for tolerance towards minorities is every more strongly raised, this can only lead to a social practice that appears to integrate these social minorities while in fact excluding them more sharply than before. The ideology of homosexual equality, quite unperturbed by actual differences and non-equalities, makes homosexuals into compulsive imitators of normality, without enabling them to bridge the chasm that actually separates them from this. The final result would be that every single person expresses tolerance for homosexuals, yet in a completely abstract sense, so that the old hostility takes its revenge and resurges as soon as there is any confrontation with those aspects of homosexual life that really are different.

The extent to which homosexuals are prepared to act in the ways demanded of them is shown by their moralising self-denial of those elements that make homosexuality 'deviant'. Above all, this involves the forms of sexual practice customary in many subcultural fields, these being denied even by those who participate in them. The same propensity is also shown in the hatred expressed towards those who either cannot or will not conceal their homosexuality.[4] In order to deserve the blessings of tolerance, homosexuals act as if they really were equal, or as if they had managed to renounce any behaviour that this tolerance does not tolerate. It is possible that a mimicry of this kind brings greater integration into society. This need not involve frequenting the homosexual subculture any the less.[5] Yet it does mean that the qualitative significance of the subculture undergoes a change. A homosexual who feels integrated in the non-homosexual context, even if unable to satisfy his sexual needs there, has less motivation to seek out the subculture, and this motivation is of less social importance than was formerly the case. More than before, the subculture becomes a vacuous refuge, in which nothing more than just sex is possible.[6]

In conditions such as these, and they are now very widespread, it is still impossible to abandon the subculture and the needs it caters for, since the way sexual demand is satisfied, if at all, is one of the preconditions for social integration. (I shall go into this question in more detail later on). In order to break down the separation between social aspects and a sexual sphere that is purged of any social aspects, a separation which is forced on the subculture but also perpetuated by it,[7] a completely different kind of tolerance would be required than that presently offered. What is needed is a tolerance which would enable homosexuals to accept even that homosexual practice which departs in the most striking ways from the general ideas about love and sexuality. Whatever the particular case may be, e.g. a large number of sexual partners, or fleeting sexual contacts in murky corners, people must come to view their sexual practice as genuinely part of themselves, if they are to gain access to something they experience as alien. A breakdown of the taboo on homosexuality which stops short at recognising homosexuals as they really are and accepts them only as homosexual heterosexuals, so to speak, only reinforces their feelings of inferiority and the resulting compulsion to seek compensation in apparently misguided rituals. If liberal sexual research refuses to discuss the specificities of both heterosexuals and homosexuals, it can only contribute to a de-homosexualising of homosexuals, and supports a tendency that differs only in degree from open hostility.

11. The Specific Homosexual Biography

Any investigation of homosexual life will bring to light a specific collective biography, so long as children are reared in such a way as to produce a majority of compulsive heterosexuals and a minority of compulsive homosexuals. A theory of homosexuality has to examine this specific biography, its causes and functions. What it brings to light in the way of significant differences is in no way the predestined fate of an eternal social minority. Difference is constituted in the concrete context that society provides for individual development, generating structures that function with a certain regularity.

If we are serious in assuming an interaction between individual life history and the prevailing social context, the results of research into homosexuality must be examined from two directions. The first question that arises is the extent to which these empirical findings are influenced by the situation of homosexuals as a social minority and the stigma imposed on them. There is then the question of the extent to which features of collective homosexual existence are attributable to certain 'deficiencies' at early stages of development. This double question assumes that the specific homosexual biography, on which the results of empirical investigations permit no serious doubt, is determined by both these factors. The two zones of social impact on the homosexual cannot of course be isolated from one another in practice, since they stand in a relationship of mutual interaction and are both invariably present in their result, the adult homosexual. The difficulties that this presents, however, should not prevent us from seeking to trace the genesis of the specific biography as far back as possible in life experience.

Since what is different about homosexuals is particularly evident in the sphere of sexuality, it is particularly their forms of sexual behaviour that have called forth various interpretations. For this reason, I shall attempt here to grasp more precisely the mechanisms on which the forms of sexuality characteristic of at least a large number of homosexuals are based. Contemporary discussion is dominated by two rival approaches in explaining the forms of sexual behaviour characteristic of the subculture. The sexuality of homosexuals is seen as determined either by the patterning of their sexual drive, or alternatively by the social discrimination they experience. While the former approach, despite occasional reference to the social fate of homosexuals, sees sexual drive as determining later sexual behaviour, the second approach is based on the assumption that the striking features of homosexual reality are essentially the result of the particular social position of homosexuals.

The former approach, deriving from psychoanalysis, in one variant or another dominated discussion in Germany until quite recently. The second approach developed out of a branch of American social psychology that has governed research into 'deviance' for a long time, known as the 'labelling approach', and has spread to West Germany in recent years. Rüdiger Lautmann has taken up this labelling theory and used it for research on homosexuality, directly applying it to certain particularly striking aspects of homosexual life.[1] He assumes 'that it is in all probability the process of social stigmatisation that drives homosexuals away from relationships and into an anonymous subculture'.[2] In this way, Lautmann seeks to explain the phenomenon of sexual promiscuity that is often encountered among homosexuals, and to refute the previously current interpretation of this phenomenon. He criticises earlier sexual research for dealing in a one-sided way with the 'high number of partners and unstable relationships', since its structure of assumptions led it to see the whole problem as lying 'in the individual affected, and not in the society which originally defined this characteristic as abnormal'.[3]

I would agree with Lautmann's critique in so far as it applies to psychocentric interpretations. Psychoanalytically oriented sexual research, in particular, has paid insufficient attention to the particular social position of homosexuals, even when it has argued in socio-psychological terms. The reason why its reference to 'social oppression' does not come to grips with the underlying problem is not that the social factor influencing the phenomenon of a 'high number of partners and unstable relationships' is to be sought in the lack of subsumption by such an eminent institution of social control as marriage, rather than in social discrimination.[4] It remains very doubtful, however, whether the concept of stigma, which Lautmann seems to take as the only category adequate for investigating the modes of homosexual behaviour, does justice to the phenomenon in question. Stigma is a purely interactionist concept, it 'describes a process in which certain individuals are visibly branded as morally inferior, for instance by way of prejudicial description and evaluation or by publicly disseminated information'.[5] Lautmann in fact restricts the effective field of social constraint on individual biography still more than the psychoanalysis he criticises. In his conception, social forces only intervene in the life of homosexuals when they are in a position to perceive themselves as such. This is because the pernicious process of stigmatisation, i.e. the negative sanctioning and proscription of certain social behaviour, can only occur when that behaviour has already made its appearance. Even self-stigmatisation can only be effective if the individual in question is able to perceive himself as a homosexual and thus as belonging to a negatively sanctioned group. Since Lautmann simply rejects psychoanalysis, without any discussion of its findings, he falls back behind the level this has managed to reach. By refusing any analysis of the stages of development that precede the definitive manifestation of homosexuality, he finds himself forced to explain the striking aspects of homosexual behaviour simply in terms of the social reaction to it.

I would not contest the influence of social deprecation on the behaviour of homosexuals, which Lautmann emphasises.[6] But nothing is gained if a trenchant critique of psychocentric interpretations of the homosexual phenomenon leads to the abandonment of all psychology whatsoever, and the dynamic of individual drive is dismissed as unimportant. By renouncing any discussion of individual life experience before the moment when the disposition to homosexuality acquired in earlier stages of development becomes manifest, the force of the taboo on homosexuality is markedly underestimated. Unintentionally, therefore, the individual is deprived of a dimension of his subjectivity. If the specific modes of homosexual behaviour and the structure of the homosexual subculture are one-sidedly conceived as simply the result of social deprecation, then in the best of cases what is analysed is the palpable and manifest taboo that holds sway over those who perceive themselves as homosexual and behave accordingly. The more general taboo on homosexuality, however, intervenes much earlier on in individual development. It leaves scars and symptoms that make themselves felt at the stage of coming out as a homosexual or even later,[7] even though their origin lies far back behind this stage.

Homosexual desires do not just come into conflict with social norms when homosexuals are ascribed a negative social role; they also come into conflict with the cultural demand for heterosexual functioning that is anchored in the individual psyche, i.e. with the mental side of the taboo. It is this mental aspect and its internalisation that give the social deprecation its threatening character, such that it can put individual identity in question. The social rejection of homosexuals may well provoke and reinforce self-deprecation, but this is already implanted at the various stages of socialisation prior to coming out, so that social rejection cannot be its cause. Naturally, this self-deprecation can only erupt with full force if the individual in question perceives himself as a homosexual. Without anyone else being aware of this, and thus before any deliberate and manifest sanction can be imposed, homosexual self-recognition leads to a general insecurity and conscious guilt. Through the pernicious interaction between the internalised taboo on homosexuality and the general sanctioning (stigmatising) of homosexuals, the mere reading of an anti-homosexual passage in the Bible, for example, can be sufficient occasion for a violent internal conflict, and a temporary renunciation of the attempt to realise homosexual desires.[8]

A socio-political conception which approaches the conflicts of homosexuals only via a concept that ignores the life experience preceding the definitive manifestation of homosexuality will not meet its own claim of disclosing 'the structure and processes of this intolerable stigma', 'so that social change can be undertaken in the interest of the free and dignified development of a minority'.[9] If present indications are not deceptive, then a de-stigmatisation within the present social system would not seem ruled out. An outcome of this kind, however, could scarcely lead to a free and dignified development such as Lautmann has in mind. The dignified development of homosexuals needs more than a social organisation that abandons its additional, institutionally anchored and palpable stigmatisation of homosexuals, yet still tenderly defends the mental aspect of the taboo on homosexuality, which remains as it has always been an unchallenged component of socialisation in our culture.

A comparison of the number of sexual partners between homosexual and heterosexual men seems at first sight to confirm the hypothesis that the high number of homosexual partners is a direct result of social deprecation. Of the students questioned by Giese and Schmidt, those in the highest age range (26-30) showed the following numbers of sexual partners since their first sexual experience:[10]

    83% up to 10
    9% 11 to 20
    7% more than 20.

The homosexual men questioned by Reimut Reiche and myself, on the other hand, gave the following picture:

    11% up to 10
    9% 11 to 20
    80% more than 20.

A comparison of present sexual behaviour also shows the high number of partners for homosexual men. According to Schmidt and Sigusch, only 17% of male unmarried workers, and 6% of students, had more than 6 female sexual partners in the previous 12 months.[11] In our survey of homosexual men, one in seven turned out to have had sex with more than 50 men in the previous year, which led us to view such high numbers as normal.[12]

Even if the empirical data presented here can only be compared with certain qualifications, firstly because the two surveys were separated by several years and secondly because they may be distorted by a different age distribution, they still show quite clearly a far greater degree of 'promiscuity' among homosexual men, a fact that is scarcely contested any longer in sexual research, and is customarily ascribed to 'social stigma'.

Yet a comparison of number of partners between homosexual men and homosexual women casts a different light. The basis for this comparison is given by the empirical data from a survey of homosexual women made by Schäfer and Schmidt,[13] and the data produced by Reimut Reiche and myself and rearranged in relation to age distribution.[14] There is a striking difference between the two groups. Whereas only 1% of homosexual women had more than 10 different sexual partners in the year prior to the survey, this was the case with 61% of homosexual men.[15]

These results indicate that the criterion of 'sexual stigma' is too crude to give a satisfactory explanation for the striking way in which homosexual men are distinguished from both heterosexual men and homosexual women. Even if homosexual women are stigmatised in a different way than homosexual men, we cannot assume that the degree of stigma is so much lower as to explain the discrepancy. If it really were simply the social persecution that determined the high number of partners for homosexual men, then the number of partners for homosexual women should still be nearer to these than to heterosexual men or women.[16]

Lautmann's idea that social stigma drives homosexual men out of relationships and into the subculture and promiscuity is also based on the rigid idea that a love relationship between homosexuals is incompatible with more frequent sexual contact with third parties. This however is refuted by the actual practice of many homosexual men. Frequent sexual contact with third parties is nothing out of the ordinary for homosexual lovers.[17] And if the social stigma manifested in the negative attitude of the population, and the social control deriving from it, does not prevent more than half of all homosexual men from having love relationships at any given time, and almost two-fifths of these sharing a home with their lover,[18] it is hard to understand why this same stigma — which at least in this respect is successfully opposed — should drive a large section of those homosexuals who have lovers into additional casual contacts. The contradiction here indicates that the behaviour of homosexuals is decisively influenced by factors that do not arise from the social discrimination against them but pertain to a sphere which we are accustomed to call the subjective factor.

M.S. Weinberg and C.J. Williams are more resolute even than Lautmann in conducting their empirical investigation without reference to subjective factors and the pressures resulting from these.[19] Their study, conducted as a cross-cultural comparison between homosexuals in the USA, Holland and Denmark, assumes a mechanical relationship between the degree of social tolerance or hostility, and the behaviour and problems of homosexuals. The central hypothesis of Weinberg and Williams is that the differing degree of tolerance towards homosexuals in the societies under investigation has a direct effect on their psychosocial constitution.

Even assuming that individual psychosocial constitution could be adequately grasped from empirical studies of this kind, and with the concepts that Weinberg and Williams deploy, the results they present are crushing for the interactionist perspective:

> In our cross-cultural comparisons, the model we employ points to different homosexual lifestyles and differences in the degree and kind of problems homosexuals face as the result of differences in the societal reaction to homosexuality. Due to more rejection, in general, one would expect American homosexuals to have more psychological problems than their European counterparts. Our data, however, provide no support for such reasoning . . . We argue (and the data suggest) that there are no major differences among the three societies with regard to our respondents' psychological problems, despite differences in the socio-cultural reactions to homosexuals.[20]

Despite the obvious difference in the level of tolerance or rejection of homosexuals between the countries investigated in this study,[21] the authors have to admit that problems pertaining to the 'social nature' of homosexuality exist in all three societies.[22] One of the reasons for this result that surprised the authors is sought in the dependence of the subculture on the level of legal and social repression. On the one hand, a high degree of repression may make for a thriving subculture, with the help of which the homosexual may be able to resolve or at least compensate for a part of his problems. On the other hand, the removal of legal repression, together with a greater tolerance on the part of the population, may bring with it a more far-reaching integration into society, accompanied by a disintegration or disorganisation of the homosexual subculture. The ensuing reduction in the possibilities of compensation may explain, according to Weinberg and Williams, the presence of 'psychological' problems in homosexuals even in societies with a greater level of tolerance.[23]

These observations are based on a quite undialectical notion of the dependence of the homosexual subculture on the surrounding society. There is no linear relationship between the integration of homosexuals into society and their integration into the subculture. This is already shown by the way that older homosexuals display a low level of subcultural participation, without it being possible to assume that this betokens a stronger integration outside of the subculture. Their lack of integration lies rather in the laws of the subculture itself. With a one-dimensional view of the homosexual subculture that sees this simply as the result of legal discrimination and social hostility, it is impossible to grasp its specific dynamic. Among other things, this always offers an organisational context for those forms of interaction which meet the immediate 'needs' of homosexuals better than the corresponding institutions of the surrounding society. The subculture is not just an instrument for evading social sanctions. Even in its present form, it is more than a dug-out in which people take refuge in order to survive the anti-homosexual bombardment. Within it, forms of sexuality are displayed, and interests articulated, that add a new layer of difference to the formal deviation of homosexuality. For this reason, it does not die away when social repression is absent or significantly reduced. The experience of recent years in West Germany, since the modification of paragraph 175, indicates a relationship between subculture and anti-homosexual repression that quite contradicts the view which would one-sidedly reduce the basis of the subculture to social hostility.

The initial modification of the law on homosexuality did not in any way weaken the organised homosexual subculture. The very opposite was the case. While up to 1969 such typical institutions of the homosexual subculture as sauna clubs were absent from the homosexual subculture in West Germany, soon every town of any size came to have such an establishment. The removal of legal repression, or at least a relative relaxation in enforcing anti-homosexual laws together with a more liberal popular attitude, has nowhere yet led to any disorganisation or elimination of the subculture. In periods of tolerance, this expands precisely in those spheres that seem to offer casual sexual contact. The 'liberalisation' of recent years has led to a growth in establishments where the cover of normality is thinner than in the traditional bars, and which are both more comfortable and at the same time better protected than the traditional meeting-places for casual encounters.[24]

In periods marked by a decline in anti-homosexual repression and an only partial subordination to the social norm, the specific difference in homosexual behaviour that derives from a mental compulsion presents itself more clearly than otherwise. What was previously unable to reach the surface of social consciousness, being prevented from revealing itself by the anti-homosexual repression, is now trapped by the levelling grip of integration, and stopped from manifesting itself in another way. This applies in particular to homosexual promiscuity, which bears more clearly than other phenomena that depart from the general norm the mark of determination by individual drive. If homosexuals have difficulty in attaining what they seem to desire, i.e. 'a lasting relationship with a single partner',[25] this has its decisive cause overwhelmingly in the mental aspect of homosexual existence.

The refusal by Weinberg and Williams to recognise this aspect of compulsion, and their one-sided attempt to explain the 'psychological problems' of homosexuals in terms of social reaction, recoils against their own argument. The subject, who is brushed aside in their explanatory model, finds a way of return in their own empirical results.

The findings presented by Weinberg and Williams not only refute the mechanical hypothesis with which they started (greater hostility = more problems/greater tolerance = fewer problems). These results also go against all the efforts of sociologically oriented sexual research to eliminate the mental aspect from homosexual behaviour. The mental and the social are inseparably bound together here. For the items 'self-acceptance, psychomatic symptoms, depression, anxiety, shame, etc.'[26] that Weinberg and Williams deploy in their investigation of 'psychological problems' not only uncover disturbances that are the result of the social reaction to homosexuals in the zone of secondary socialisation; they also disclose deeper-lying conflicts deriving from primary socialisation. Naturally, these conflicts too are not free from the influence of society. What persists in them are the mental precipitates of the contradiction between heterosexuality and homosexuality that is constantly recreated by 'cultural normality'. What psychoanalysis calls 'subjectivity' does not involve simply the experience of a particular mother-child relationship. The homosexual mind also bears the signs of a collective socialisation that cannot be simply shrugged off, a process that is designed to inhibit homosexuality and promote heterosexuality. The precipitates of this collective experience belong to deeper and more resistant levels of the human mind than the experiences resulting from the social persecution of homosexuals and its effects.

For this reason, therefore, the 'psychological problems' of homosexuals do not disappear in a climate of greater tolerance. This social trend only affects, at least initially, the 'external' position of homosexuals; tolerance improves their social position, alleviates social adaptation and in this way also pacifies the mental conflicts in some respects. The differential sanctioning of homosexuality established by Weinberg and Williams is expressed in their results most clearly at this level. Among the American homosexuals, only a quarter of those questioned were not worried about their homosexuality being known, anticipated only minor discrimination as a result of this and concealed their homosexuality only to a minor degree. In those European countries defined as more tolerant, on the other hand, more than half of those questioned fell in this group.[27] It follows from this that it is certainly worthwhile working to expand the limits of tolerance, and that it would be foolish to impugn what can be attained in this way. Yet it is still necessary to guard against the illusions that are inherent to the interactionist perspective.

12. Deviance and Social Adaptation

Sociologically oriented sexual research of the kind mentioned above depends, as I have sought to show, on ignoring those disturbances deriving from primary socialisation and on denying the unconscious desires and compulsions these involve. In so far as it does deal in any way with the manifestations of unconscious desires, it sees these manifestations solely as collective defence strategies against external dangers arising from social reality. Little violence is done to this kind of sexual research if its underlying assumption is summed up as follows: If there were no social discrimination against homosexuals, there would be no specifically homosexual modes of behaviour. Whenever research into homosexuality is conducted in the 'perspective of the definitional approach that has now become current in sociology'[1], i.e. the labelling approach, the attempt is made at a social psychology that does not get too deeply psychological.[2] The popularity of labelling theory is due in large part to an insufficient reflection by the psychoanalytic theory of 'deviance' on those social compulsions that are active subsequent to the early stages of socialisation. And to this extent labelling theory contains a just response to the inadequate understanding of the behaviour of social minorities in this traditional theory.

According to H.S. Becker's *Sociology of Deviant Behaviour*, such behaviour is 'not a quality inherent in the behaviour itself, but rather in the interaction between a person who acts and others who react'.[3] The specific homosexual biography that so impresses the sociologist would thus be constituted from the institutionalised expectation of other people as mediated via a ramified system of interaction.[4] At the start of such a process of interaction, accordingly, there is an action conceived as neutral and value-free:

> If we direct our attention to behaviour characterised as deviant, we have to recognise that we only know whether a given action is to be considered deviant or not when it is followed by the reaction of others to it.[5]

If the specific biography of homosexuals is to be reconstructed by the application of Becker's proposed theoretical model, we start with a homosexual act or at least with information about someone's homosexuality, to which other people subsequently react. The original actor reacts in turn to this reaction, and so on. But since we can only conceive of negative reactions to acts commonly characterised as deviant, or in the best of cases benignly neutral reactions — certainly never positive[6] — the interaction sets in motion a process in the course of which a repertoire of behaviour is constructed that is typical of the group in question and strikes us as deviant.

This already displays the formalistic character of labelling theory. Its conceptual vocabulary does not permit any statement about the third step in the interaction process, i.e. the reaction of the original actor, now identified as deviant, to the reaction that follows his original action or identification. Even given an immediate and violently negative sanctioning of the original action, both the reaction to the sanction and its effect are dependent to a considerable extent on the personality of the individual affected. The person who suffers a negative sanction in everyday life is not just a mere victim. Nor can he be seen as a blank surface on which sanctions are inscribed like a programme. The interaction theory, then, if it does not completely overlook the active contribution people make to their own destiny, at least reduces this to so minimal a role as to produce an image that degrades the human being to an unresisting object of social norms.

The model proposed by Becker is totally unsuited to elucidate the motivations and impulses underlying those actions which do not follow the prescribed social rules. It is impossible to isolate a moment in time at which all behaviour is deemed equal, with judgements suddenly changing in such a way as to reveal by the reactions of others the social verdict on a specific action. Behavioural expectations are in fact formulated in advance by the prevailing social organisation. Anyone who is even half grown-up — and this is generally the case even with 'deviant minorities' — knows that his action is deviant before he commits it; he does not have to wait for the reaction of other people. In our present society the taboo on homosexuality has a collective presence and has been internalised by all of society's members, if to a varying extent. This means, then, that everyone has a vague feeling telling them: You must not do anything homosexual. This feeling is reconfirmed by the negative reactions to a particular homosexual act or to identification as a homosexual, but the feeling does not originate simply with the negative sanctions, which means that only relatively mild sanctions are needed.

At least with those social norms that make a totalitarian demand — and the compulsion to heterosexuality is certainly one of these — reactions to any intended 'deviant' act are always anticipated in advance. What may be experienced by particular groups and individuals in the interaction process is in this respect secondary, and largely a matter of degree. The fact that a specific negative reaction to homosexuality is not required for the selection of a particular path through life is evident at the coming-out stage. At this stage, actual or intended homosexual activity is inhibited far more by fantasies than by concrete sanctions. The individual in question imagines the most violent negative reactions to a homosexual act that he has in mind, reactions that are never paralleled by the actual sanctions encountered, and these fantasised reactions have a far more decisive effect on his biography. What is determinant for the life of a homosexual outsider is in fact not at all reactions to certain actions that are mistakenly seen as inherently neutral, but rather certain mental dispositions involving desires and inclinations. These dispositions more or less obstinately compel certain modes of behaviour and rule out others, which can lead in a given society to conflicts with social institutions and with individuals as the representatives of social norms.[7]

How inconsequential stigmatisation is for the formation of a specifically homosexual biography when it cannot build on appropriate mental dispositions already in place is shown by those cases when individuals are branded as homosexual by legal condemnation on the grounds of a single chance encounter. Despite this stigmatisation by the highest authority, they in no way become homosexuals as a result. Those branded in this way may possibly become 'criminal' outsiders; but in order to become homosexual outsiders, other preconditions must be already in place besides mere homosexual behaviour.[8]

In order to reach a more comprehensive understanding of the modes of homosexual behaviour than is possible with the approach of modern sexual research, it is necessary to turn to individual homosexuals themselves, even if without forgetting their position as outsiders. This, however, means leaving behind the position of liberal sexual research, seemingly so well-disposed towards homosexuals, and which, in contrast to psychoanalysis, has enjoyed such favour among them. This favour results from the deep affinity which exists between the current self-interpretation of homosexuals and the interpretation of homosexual behaviour by liberal sexual research. Both parties proceed as if to excuse homosexuals for their offence and reapportion the blame to society, which Guy Hocquenghem calls 'a falsely progressive position which turns out to be even more ruthless towards homosexuals than open repression'.[9] With this observation he chastises both the constraints to which homosexuals are subject, and their own readiness to subject their sexual and other needs to an indifferent sexual morality.

The empty formula that society is to blame for certain modes of behaviour seems to correspond to a widespread need among homosexuals. On the one hand, it confirms their identification with the current notions of sexual morality. If this identification were not made, there would be no cause to apologise and seek to shift the blame to society. On the other hand, this formula excuses all those who, despite their identification with the moral ideas of the present society, still behave differently from how they are told. The refuge taken in this formula feeds the idea that homosexuals are fundamentally good and are only prevented from expressing their goodness by social stigma. This involves ignoring at least two characteristics of real individuals. The loose expression that society is to blame is indifferent both to the pain of those who suffer on account of their 'subjectivity' and to the benefit they may well derive from modes of behaviour that their own morality leads them to despise. They are thus encouraged to a pessimistic and resigned attitude to their problems. The subjective suffering, whether on account of the forms of homosexual relationship or the compulsive search for casual sexual contacts, is concealed; it can no longer give any impetus for change. Given the greater power of the social order, any remonstration against this suffering must seem fruitless, and so people go on behaving as this idea says they have to behave. They are not particular individual subjects with concrete desires and fantasies, with anxieties, dislikes and phobias, who commit or omit particular actions within a concrete society; it is rather an immediate social force that determines what they do and what they don't do, quite irrespective of the desires and strengths of those involved. Anyone who believes that he acts as he does solely on account of the compulsions inflicted by secondary socialisation will never struggle either against the compulsion anchored in his individual mind nor against the compulsions of the external world.

13. Homosexuality as a Psychological Phenomenon

By emphasising here the mental aspect of homosexual behaviour, I do not in any way intend to rekindle the old debate as to whether homosexuality is pathological. This insistence on psychology results rather from the conviction that the 'damaged identity' of homosexual subjects can only be understood by using this particular instrument of knowledge. Naturally, any procedure of this kind runs the risk of discovering potentials for disturbance that lie 'in the personality of those affected'. As regards the question of pathology, I view manifest homosexuality as a specific resolution for conflicts of early childhood, which must be seen as having a meaning in its own terms, i.e. in the context of life experience. Homosexuality is essentially comparable with other ways of resolving infantile disturbances that lurk behind a formal heterosexuality. Viewed psychologically, there are only quantitative differences between homosexuality and heterosexuality, and not qualitative ones. If homosexuality is accepted at this level, there is no sense in calling it pathological. Homosexuality is just as little or much a sickness as is heterosexuality, though this in no way means that a fair number of homosexuals do not exhibit mental disturbances. If homosexuality is subjected to an immanent analysis, i.e. an analysis oriented to its specific laws, we have to ask whether and to what extent it achieves what it is basically capable of achieving, i.e. mental well-being and the capacity to operate in society, and this means mental health in the context of homosexuality. If we are not to fall into a vacuous functionalism, however, we have to give an account of the conditions under which homosexuality takes on this identity-defining role.

In an essay of great importance for the theory of homosexuality, Fritz Morgenthaler comes to the conclusion that a symptom 'which when viewed laterally is pathological and can be attributed to certain deficiencies at particular stages of development, may present the best solution for an optimal interaction between the mental systems and the self when viewed longtitudinally, i.e. in terms of the total development of the personality'.[1] Morgenthaler seeks to understand sexual perversions and homosexuality as 'ego-achievements of a particular kind'.[2] He stresses the functional aspect of such forms of conflict resolution, i.e. the aspect oriented to adaptation, and he is in fact quite fascinated by the identity-defining function of perverse symptoms. Where homosexuality does not fulfil the expectation of taking up the inheritance of early childhood in a relatively disturbance-free manner, and some kind of therapy is indicated, then the aim of psychoanalytic treatment is to establish conditions that facilitate the optimal interaction Morgenthaler refers to. He is in fact extremely critical of ideas which see therapeutic success in simple terms of overcoming homosexuality. He sees rigorous therapeutic measures of the kind expounded by Socarides as an unanalytic procedure. The behaviour of those colleagues of his who view the aim of therapy as getting rid of homosexuality or a perversion, he sees as inspired less by psychoanalytic doctrine than by a blind identification with anti-homosexual social structures:

If the analyst expects the process of cure to consist in the perversions, homosexuality or bisexuality dis-

appearing or giving way to 'normal' sexual objects, he
is unconsciously following the role ascribed to him by
society.[3]

Here Morgenthaler makes it unmistakeably clear that
the purpose of psychoanalysis is not to make everyone
heterosexual. Its true task is rather to help people to
operate in society and to love. Analytic practice can then
dispense with the question as to whether homosexuality is
necessarily pathological, and finally grant homosexuality
the same right that was always assumed for heterosexuality, for this too undoubtedly bears unmistakeably
pathological features in its prevalent cultural form.[4] The
relevance of this development in regard to the readiness of
homosexuals to opt for psychotherapy, in appropriate
conditions, should not be underestimated. Their justified
fear of such therapy being used to 'straighten them out'
must have stopped large numbers of homosexuals seeking
therapeutic help even when they were in need of this. The
'threshold fear' of therapy, which analysts such as
Socarides significantly increase, certainly seems to be far
greater among homosexuals than among heterosexuals.

In Morgenthaler's work, as generally in the theory of
narcissism, the strict distinction between homosexuals and
heterosexuals is dissolved, and attention is focused on
structural disturbances that can equally appear on both
sides. The emphasis here is placed on quantitative aspects,
i.e. the degree of narcissistic disturbances and others in the
development of the narcissistic sector of a personality. In
Morgenthaler's metapsychological theory, homosexuality
and the perversions are conceived as functioning like a
'seal' or 'filling', 'a heterogenous pattern that stops up the
gaps created by an inadequate narcissistic development.
Thanks to this filling, homeostasis in the narcissistic
sphere is facilitated and maintained.'[5] The quantita-

tive perspective is decisive in respect to this 'filling' as well, since a narcissistic development *without* such a 'filling' is inconceivable, even if it may be far from readily apparent.

It depends on the severity of conflicts in the early phases of development, when 'the sensitivity of the mother in her dual union with the child plays a decisive role',[6] whether the narcissistic 'filling' later takes a perverse or homosexual form.

The process leading to a perverse or homosexual filling is extremely complex,[7] and for our present purpose we can pass it over. What should be noted, however, is that in the ideal case, the prosthetic supplement is sufficiently firm in its substance that its bearers 'display, beside the accidental deviation in their sexual life, a personality development which enables them to construct and maintain libidinally invested object relations, to develop and pursue lasting interests, and their life does not display any sharp turn in its lines of developments that would have a major effect on their social relations'.[8] I should like to support Morgenthaler's conviction as to the possible positive course of a homosexual or perverse development, and I also do not doubt the existence of happy homosexuals or 'perverts' of this kind. What I cannot share, however, is his optimism with respect to the distribution of such a smooth development, as far as homosexuals are concerned. It is certainly true that only a relatively few homosexual or perverse individuals ever 'seek medical advise, let alone psychoanalytic treatment'.[9] But Morgenthaler is surely wrong in inferring from this that all those who don't turn to a doctor for help enjoy an undisturbed emotional life in the sense that he defines this. The claim of homosexuals to happiness has been seriously reduced by their long history of persecution and social discrimination. Their capacity and even their readiness for suffering has increased, for as a homosexual in this society, you always have things a little bit worse. There are undoubtedly many who have never consulted a doctor or an analyst, but who suffer mental disturbances that are hardly bearable, and which they have a consuming struggle to control.[10]

The criteria by which Morgenthaler distinguishes between healthy and disturbed emotional life, moreover, are less clear-cut than they may first appear. When he refers to the 'striking deviation in sexual life', he seems ultimately to mean nothing more than a formal deviation from the cultural ideal of normality. Homosexuality, accordingly, would be no more than a simple inversion of the sexual object, with other functions remaining normal. Other departures than the merely formal, however, such as a general or temporary inability to construct and maintain libidinally invested object relations, are frequently characteristic of the homosexual form of resolution, and show this as only partially successful. The ideal case of a successful homosexual development, at least in outward appearance, is seen as conceivable only in the shape of that celebrated homosexual who differs from a successful heterosexual development solely in his choice of sexual object. A homosexual development of this kind, however, seems at present to be reached only by those with a truly blessed nature, who combine a whole bundle of favourable circumstances.

We need further enlightenment from psychoanalysis as to the preconditions for a development of this kind. Already, however, we can say that a homosexual development free from disturbance comes up against 'social conditions' and is either destroyed by these or at least made considerably more difficult. For homosexuality as a narcissistic 'filling' must have a social as well as a mental anchorage. And this social anchorage is made more difficult by the discrimination against homosexuals, which in turn has an effect on the mental anchorage, loosening its supports. The ability to enter into stable and passionate object relations, in particular, can obviously develop only very incompletely in the context of struggle with both internal and external conflicts. If we are to follow O.F. Kernberg's criterion of normality, according to which 'only relatively normal people have the capacity for falling in love and developing such a passionate attachment into a stable love relation',[11] then empirical results show that only a small proportion of homosexuals are free from disturbances in their capacity for love. A fairly large number, on the other hand, suffer from narcissistic or neurotic disturbances so serious that neither the capacity to fall in love nor to remain in love has been able to develop.[12] The sexual promiscuity which appears in connection with these disturbances is persistent, and should be distinguished from a merely temporary promiscuity, involving a different complex of conflicts.

This problem cannot be conjured away by the fact that the depth of these conflicts may remain concealed from the homosexuals in question, as well as from empirical sexual research, since 'a temporary enthusiasm for the desired sexual object may imitate the state of falling in love'.[13] A mere fascination of this kind, only imitating the stage of falling in love, generally disappears after a short period, and frequently after the first sexual consummation; not only the sexual attraction, but all other interest as well, is shown to have been directed from the very beginning to an unconsciously devalued sham love-object. If sexual consummation is postponed for some reason, or ruled out altogether, then the victim can develop into a frenzied lover who pursues the object he simultaneously adores and hates, literally throws himself at his feet, and knows no peace until he has possessed him.

In a further configuration which Kernberg describes, and which characterised a majority of respondents in our own survey, there indeed seems to be an undisturbed ability to fall in love, and therefore a key precondition for the ability to love. But this stage of development is marked by strong ambivalences, resulting from the way that the fears emerging in relation to the sexual and love-object are at least partially conscious and can no longer be completely projected and warded off. There is not the same unconscious devaluation of the object as when there is no real falling in love in the first place. The illusion of an uninhibited capacity for love, marked by romantic idealisations, declines and crumbles away. Now it is not simply the partner who is experienced as unworthy of love. The hatred which manifests itself time and again in .elation with him, and the partial disdain for him, are experienced consciously and thus lead to unease and feelings of guilt. These feelings, however, represent a portion of hope, the hope of 'overcoming the profound unconscious devaluation of the love-object',[14] which makes the love affairs of these people so full of conflict.

Those homosexuals who have reached a stage of development marked by the capacity to fall in love, but still also by an at least partial inability to establish lasting, stable and passionate relations, are particularly susceptible to the slogan that society is to blame, and may use this to explain a behaviour that they themselves at least partially fail to comprehend. There can be no doubt that the unconsidered use of this formula bears traces of a collective rationalisation, and even when endowed with the dignity of science it still promotes an illusory interpretation of reality. But it is not only the unholy alliance between this rationalisation and the traditional idea of homosexuals as people unchangeably incapable of love that makes it harder to work through and rise out of the conflicts concealed behind this incapacity and perpetuating it. Such a resolution is further obstructed by the high degree of secondary gain from illness which brings consolation for a desire that roams aimlessly around, incapable of love. All this makes it more difficult to break out of the contradiction between the desire for intimacy and protection in a love relationship, and the more or less unconscious fears of fulfilling this desire. The key medium into which this gain from illness is converted is sexual promiscuity, and this has either an exclusive or a subsidiary character depending on the configuration of disturbances in the capacity for love.

It is immediately apparent how the fact that sexual promiscuity can become the bearer of the gain from illness makes the resolution of the conflict that much harder. In contrast to a compulsive neurotic symptom, for example, which 'comes into the patient's mental life at first as an unwelcome guest; it has everything against it'[15], remaining highly burdensome even when a certain use has been found for it, promiscuity is never such a burden and is far more closely associated with pleasure right from the start. Besides, the reason why sexual promiscuity can fulfil the tasks ascribed it by the mental economy so effectively is that in a fundamental respect it has the same function as sexuality in general, which in the case of homosexuality plays a far greater role: 'At the moment of orgasm there is a qualitative shift, with sexual satisfaction, transformed into a sense of well-being, reinforcing the representations of self and object alike.'[16]

Through orgasm, therefore, a state of mental anxiety and pain (narcissistic disharmony) is transformed into mental well-being (narcissistic harmony). Neither Socarides, who describes this process in a similar way to Morgenthaler,[17] nor Morgenthaler himself, make a distinction in this process between casual sexual contacts and sexual experiences integrated into a love relationship. What is decisive for the transformation effect is as it were simply orgasm with a male partner. I maintained above that sexuality cannot assume any fundamentally different function for homosexuals than it has in general, and that the different here is solely quantitative. But I must still insist that homosexual contacts generally do serve to a far greater extent the purpose of defence against phenomena of mental dissolution and disintegration than is normal for heterosexual contacts. This shift of emphasis arises, according to Morgenthaler, because 'the perverse[18] individual has no structured defence organisation at his disposal, such as would enable him to combat breakthroughs of emotion otherwise than by a sexual emergency function, the perversion'[19] i.e., for the homosexual, homosexual activity.[20]

In the extreme case, this quantitative shift is almost qualitative in its effects. For manifest homosexuality, like the perversions, involves a change in the function of sexual satisfaction, on which the reintegration effects achieved through sexual contact are themselves dependent. What homosexuals, like other people, generally see as the primary goal of their sexual encounters, i.e. pleasure and sexual satisfaction, is not really what is fundamental:

> What the perverse individuals seek to achieve in their sexual goals, and what they insist on with extreme stubbornness, is in no way the satisfaction of sexual drive, but rather the preservation of their desexual-ised object relations, their aim-inhibited tender feelings, their ideals and ambitions in the social context in which they live and to which they have

adapted. The self-esteem of the perverse, their feelings of identity, including their sexual role as well, are quite decisively dependent on the preservation of all those ego-functions and libido investments that — as if severed from the sexual syndrome of the perversion — have been formed in the entire development of their personality. It is important for the analyst to know that what the patient depicts as the satisfaction of sexual drive has in fact a different significance: the change of function involved in drive activity is so much to the fore that the satisfaction of sexual drive in itself is not only secondary, but in most cases given remarkably little investment and undervalued. It is almost a matter of indifference.[21]

At first sight, the wealth of tasks with which homosexuality is burdened appear confusing. On the one hand, it has to take on the main work of the defensive struggle against breakthroughs of emotion that threaten the mental balance. On the other hand, it has a decisive share in the preservation of a whole series of mental functions. Yet this confusing plethora of tasks is subordinate to a single goal: to maintain and restore a mental identity that is always in danger, and in this way also to achieve social adaptation in all other spheres of life.

The findings depicted above, and derived from clinical practice, can also help yield a deeper insight into the organised forms of sexuality in the homosexual subculture. We are now less helpless in the face of the high number of homosexual partners than those tempted to explain this one-sidedly in terms of the absence of an institutional constraint such as supervises the love relationships of heterosexuals. Nor need the high sexual frequency be virtually biologised, in the name of a 'strong' sexual drive, and thus abstracted away from the social context. Of course, despite this analysis of the functions of sexuality, one key question has still not been satisfactorily answered, i.e. that of the promiscuous tendencies of homosexual men. For the tasks ascribed to sexuality may be just as well fulfilled within a love relationship, and need in no way necessarily lead to promiscuity. The genesis of homosexuality is of decisive importance here. If it goes back to a disturbed narcissistic development and involves a conflict with the first love-object (the mother), this leading to an inadequate demarcation between self and object, though of course to a varying extent, then this is an inheritance every adult homosexual must enter into. It is this inheritance, however, that makes it harder to achieve that balance between intimacy and distance which alone makes a love relationship bearable.

From the arsenal of possibilities available for controlling an underlying narcissistic conflict, homosexual men have chosen flight into a temporary or permanent promiscuity, so as either to parry the anxiety induced by the intimacy of a love relationship, or else permanently to avoid it — in this respect quite comparable with a group of narcissistically disturbed heterosexual men. Homosexuals, however, cannot deal with this anxiety in the same way as those heterosexual men who solve the problem by a complete subjugation of their wives, since in homosexuality both partners ultimately remain in a masculine role, which as a general rule excludes any lasting and one-sided subordination of this kind.

If we take all these factors together, then it will I hope become clear why homosexuality has to be assessed according to its inherent mental laws and not those of a hypostatised heterosexuality. There is a traceable path leading from these mental laws to the influences of social deprecation on homosexual self-esteem. Narcissistic discordances are always inflamed by the demands of reality. Among other things, however, homosexuals are exposed to a severe and permanent narcissistic insult which takes the form of their proclaimed inferiority. This sets in motion the following train of affairs. Under the pressure of reality, disturbances arise in a narcissistic balance that is susceptible to upset, and as a reaction to this threat to mental stability 'a state of distress is proclaimed, leading to the perverse activity.'[22] Narcissistic homeostatis is subsequently reestablished through sexual contact, if only for a short while. In this interaction of the mental and social, we can see how the incriminating finger of social stigma promotes the very behaviour that, qua moral authority, it purports to prevent. The result of this process is then once again attacked by sexual morality, and the deprecation redoubled.

From what has already been said we can also understand those subcultural spheres which appear to serve no other purpose than that of rapid sexual release. For this state of distress which can brook no delay leads to an exaggeration of the sexual aspect of homosexual life, accompanied by a characteristic indifference to the quality of sexual satisfaction. Some subcultural spheres, in particular saunas, parks and public toilets, simply provide the 'organisational framework' for the satisfaction of desires and compulsions arising from the specific conflicts to which homosexuals are subject. The visitor to these places not only finds people there who seek sexual contacts with the same motivations and reduced expectations as his own. He can also feel sheltered by the prevailing forms of communication and interaction, in so far as these correspond to his momentary needs. The goal is attained when through orgasm or even a contact made only in fantasy, the disturbed narcissistic balance is restored.

There are many subcultural venues where this is the sole specific purpose.

There can only be full reciprocity between the needs of the subject and the possible satisfaction these subcultural spheres offer if the inability to enter and maintain object relations is not experienced as disturbing or if these places serve simply to offer casual sexual contacts for people who also have a love relationship. But even for those who suffer under the constraints of the subculture (which more or less clearly reflect their own compulsions), this subculture provides them with the particular kind of satisfaction that they need, thus maintaining a whole series of important mental functions.

A significant empirical fact emerging from Reimut Reiche's and my survey illustrates how sexuality intervenes to compensate for narcissistic disharmonies and, in this way facilitating the reintegration of the ego, also supports the capacity for social functioning in work and everyday life. The inadequate self-esteem expressed in a readiness to try and 'get rid' of their homosexuality through therapy is far more frequent among those who display only a small amount of homosexual activity. While only 16% of those who have sex with another man 'daily or almost daily' would like to 'get rid of' their homosexuality, this proportion steadily rises as homosexual activity falls, and with those who display homosexual activity less than 5 times per month it is far above the average.[23]

If the tasks and functions of homosexual sexuality are conceived in the sense presented here, and not belittled, the conclusion for theory and practice is somewhat paradoxical. All those sexual phenomena that are most disparaged as particularly strange and striking, and are rejected even by the moral consciousness of homosexuals themselves, should be protected from this general deprecation. As long as the meaning concealed in these sexual phenomena is not understood, a meaning that is distorted by social deprecation and moralising self-denial, there will be no chance of providing a route by which the compulsions concealed in these forms can come to light and be treated. Morgenthaler tells of a homosexual patient for whom the 'validation of his sexual symptoms... helped to strengthen his self-esteem'[24], and how decisive this step was for the analytic process. Of course this can only be one step towards the goal, and not the goal itself. But this step, with which the contradictions between behaviour (for example the mutual deprecation expressed in compulsive promiscuity) and desires (for protection and love) as well as illusions (as to one's capacity for love), are for the moment appeased in favour of a strengthened self-esteem, can be followed by the next step, in which these contradictions are taken up and dealt with.

Up to a certain point, the homosexual subculture achieves this validation of sexual symptoms, if only through the reciprocal identification of its members. This is why any general condemnation of the subculture is so deadly. The regressive aspect of the homosexual subculture lies simply in the way that it is unaffected by this validation, that it inscribes this validation through the forms of satisfaction and communication that are already in place, and thus holds back those contradictions that not only require the validation of these particular sexual forms but also press beyond them. The structure of the subculture conceals access to the conflicts that are constitutive of the subcultural existence and makes it more difficult to deal with them, i.e. those conflicts that make more difficult, if they do not prevent entirely, love relationships that genuinely do promise happiness, that are passionate and more than just casual. Viewed from this point of view, moreover, it appears sensible to interpret the subculture in terms of a series of steps, according to the closeness or distance that is allowed or enforced by the prevailing forms of communication. At one end of the scale would then be the bars and private subcultural activities, at the other end cottages (public toilets), and in between such zones as saunas and parks. All these share, if in differing degrees, a positive sanctioning of casual sexual contacts, and a tabooing of the needs for intimacy and love that is born of fear.

14. The Superior Homosexual

The above notes on the potential for emotional disturbance to which homosexuals are liable should not be read as legitimating a general interpretation of homosexuality as 'absence and substitution'.[1] The intention of discussing the damage suffered by homosexual subjects should rather be conceived as directed against the concealment of a portion of social reality in the name of homosexuals themselves. The fact that disturbances of the capacity for love seem to be more closely associated with homosexuality than with heterosexuality says nothing about any qualitative difference between these two forms of sexuality, simply a quantitative difference, and one which, to judge from the ever greater spread of narcissistic disturbances among heterosexuals, is becoming smaller all the time. On the other hand, however, we should guard against a view that would play down the misery of homosexuals, simply because the concepts of absence and substitution can be applied to heterosexuals too. Those who go to the lengths of Guy Hocquenghem, that brilliant critic of mendacious morality and false tolerance, and view heterosexuality as a generally inferior form of sexuality, may at best help homosexuals to gain a certain elite consciousness and this make many things easier to bear, but they do not actually change anything.

Hocquenghem, appealing to the polymorphous perversity of desire, would have it that 'homosexual love is immensely superior, precisely because everything is possible at any moment: organs look for each other and plug in, unaware of the law of exclusive disjunction'.[2] Anyone who argues in this way, and asks whether homosexuals are not ultimately more healthy, must accept that he is arguing from a position of weakness, maintaining the idea of health in the homosexual context while at the same time admitting the increased potential for disturbance in the capacity for love that is so clearly present in the forms of intercourse characteristic of the homosexual subculture. Hocquenghem does not champion the specific character of homosexual love in order to combat its forcible subordination to an ideology of love that remains external to it.[3] Instead of this he constructs a new, independent and superior system of sexual desire from that portion of homosexual existence marked by promiscuity.[4] He argues, therefore, for a form of sexuality characterised by a far sharper division than that which he criticises, this not necessarily involving a compulsive separation between the object of affection and the object of sensuality. By hypostatising one particular aspect of the homosexual phenomenon, he ends up apologising for the blind mechanisms of the homosexual subculture, whose compulsions he naively celebrates, and ultimately ends up praising what is a typically masculine way of handling sexuality.

Seeing the 'mechanical scattering' (his description of the 'homosexual pick-up machine') as superior, Hocquenghem is concerned to give his system a viable basis. It is only consistent, then, that he should ontologise this system and seek to root it in a new sexual anthropology:

If the homosexual pick-up machine, which is infinitely more direct and less guilt-induced than the complex system of 'civilised loves' (to use Fourier's phrase), were to take off the Oedipal cloak of morality under which it is forced to hide,[5] we would see that *its mechanical scattering corresponds to the mode of existence of desire itself.*[6]

What distinguishes Hocquenghem from his predecessors who sought refuge in anthropology is the imperious character of his ideas. Others proposed a system of categories in which homosexuality, too, could be subsumed, but for Hocquenghem all sexuality is guilty unless it follows the ramblings of mechanical scattering: 'Aschenbach's drift around Venice is connected with a guilty sexuality because it is identified with a single object, the principle being "you lose one person and the world become empty".'[7] Yet the psychoanalysis that Hocquenghem so vigorously attacks is far less dogmatic than he is. It could reply that an object relation of this kind is not 'guilty', because it is senseless to discuss sexual behaviour in terms of guilt; but it is immature, being governed by narcissistic and neurotic elements, which is why the loss of the love-object is followed not by sadness, but by melancholia or death.

Just as there is no justification, other than an ideological one, for extrapolating a transhistorical essense of sexuality and love from the present forms of heterosexuality, so there is similarly no way that this can be derived from the forms of the homosexual subculture. To attempt to derive a superior sexual system from the most striking forms of homosexuality is to fall back behind positions already achieved. It is neither historically nor theoretically plausible to interpret homosexuality as per se superior or inferior. The only task we can set ourselves today is to bring about social conditions that will enable more homosexuals to develop in a way that homosexuality itself does not prevent. These conditions include a climate that permits us to recognise the precipitates of social contradictions in homosexual subjects, without being accused of homophobia. But when homosexuals are seen as genuine subjects, then their sufferings, their capacities and their unconscious desires are also taken seriously and as capable of change.

Notes

Preface to the English Edition

1 M. Dannecker and R. Reiche, *Der gewöhnliche Homosexuelle – Eine soziologische Untersuchung über männliche Homosexuelle in der Bundesrepublik*, Frankfurt, 1974. A summary in English of some of the findings of this survey can be found in R. Reiche and M. Dannecker, 'Male Homosexuality in West Germany – A Sociological Investigation', in *Journal of Sex Research*, vol. 13, 1, 1977.

Throughout this book, *'der Homosexuelle'*, which in German is unambiguously masculine, has been most commonly translated by the noun 'homosexual', rather than the cumbersome 'male homosexual' or 'homosexual man'. Wherever Martin Dannecker refers to lesbians as well as gay men, this has been made clear. [Translator's note.]

Preface to the German Edition

1 R. Lautmann, *Seminar: Gesellschaft und Homosexualität*, Frankfurt, 1977.

1. Legalisation and Oppression

1 See among others *Plädoyer für die Abschaffung des § 175* (with contributions from T. Brocher, A. Mergen, H. Bolewski, H.E. Müller), Frankfurt, 1966. Also H. Giese (ed.), *Homosexualität oder Politik mit dem Paragraphen 175*, Hamburg, 1967.
2 T. Brocher, 'Homosexuelles Verhalten als psychische Entwicklungsstörung', in *Plädoyer...*, loc. cit.
3 A. Mergen, 'Einspruch gegen die generelle Kriminalisierung der Homosexualität', in *Plädoyer...*, loc. cit.
4 Quoted from W. Harthauser, 'Der Massenmord an

Homosexuellen im Dritten Reich', in W.S. Schlegel (ed.), *Das grosse Tabu*, Munich, 1967, p. 22.

5 Gollner takes Rudolf Klare's work as an authentic document of the Nazi world view, on the grounds that it was expressly commissioned l y Himmler. See G. Gollner, *Homosexualität – Ideologiekritik und Entmythologisierung einer Gesetzgebung*, Berlin, 1974, p. 175.

6 R. Klare, *Homosexualität und Strafrecht*, Hamburg, 1937, p. 116.

7 G. Gollner, op. cit., p. 175.

8 P. Schröder, 'Homosexualität', in *Monatsschrift für Kriminalbiologie und Strafrechtsreform*, 1940, 10-11, p. 221.

9 T. Lang, 'Bemerkungen zu dem Aufsatz "Homosexualität" von Prof. Dr. med. Paul Schröder', in *Monatsschrift...*, 1941, 5, p. 168.

10 'The centrepiece of National Socialist legal policy is the national community. Everything that aids the nation is right, and everything that harms the nation is wrong. "The law does not ... just have the task of protecting formal values...this protection must be extended to the substantive values." Such substantive values, according to Frank, are the state, the race, the soil, labour, honour, cultural and spiritual values, and fighting power'; R. Klare, op. cit., p. 121. Klare quotes here from H. Frank, *Einleitung zum Nationalsozialistischen Handbuch für Recht und Gesetzgebung*, pp. xiii ff., Munich, 1935.

11 R. Klare, op. cit., p. 127.

12 ibid., p. 11.

13 *Bundestagsdrucksache IV 650, 4 October 1962 – Regierungsentwurf eines Strafgesetzbuches E 1962*. Quoted from *Plädoyer für die Abschaffung des § 175*, loc. cit., p. 134.

14 ibid., p. 141.

15 ibid.

16 ibid., p. 139 (emphasis M.D.).

17 R. Klare, op. cit., p. 11.

18 E 62: loc. cit., p. 132.

19 R. Klare, op. cit., p. 12.

20 E 62: loc. cit., p. 142.

21 R. Klare, op. cit., p. 12.

22 E 62: loc. cit., p. 145.

23 On this point see G. Gollner, op. cit., pp. 177 ff.

24 T. Graf and M. Steglitz, 'Homosexuellenunterdrückung in

der bürgerlichen Gesellschaft', in *Probleme des Klassenkampfs*, 1974, 4, p. 34.

25 ibid., p. 33.

26 E. Pashukanis, *Law and Marxism*, London, 1978, p. 86.

27 A. Mergen, op. cit., p. 51.

28 For a critique of behaviour therapy see M. Dannecker, 'Warum die Therapie der Homosexualität die Lage der Homosexuellen verschlechtert', in V. Sigusch (ed.), *Therapie sexueller Störungen*, Stuttgart, 1975.

29 T. Brocher, op. cit., p. 33.

30 ibid., p. 34.

31 ibid., p. 32.

32 See in particular Guy Hocquenghem, *Homosexual Desire*, London, 1978. An undialectical and ultimately biologistic treatment of damage to the subject also led sections of the gay movement to believe that 'our disability is a new and different kind of health', the logical conclusion being the desire to 'make all men gay'. (From an unpublished report by a former member of the Hamburg Schwulenbewegung HAH).

2. *Homosexuality and Anthropology*

1 A.C. Kinsey et al, 'Concepts of Normality and Abnormality in Sexual Behaviour', in P.H. Hoch and J. Zubin, *Psychosexual Development in Health and Disease*, New York, 1949, p. 27.

2 ibid.

3 ibid.

4 V.E. von Gebsattel, 'Allgemeine und medizinische Anthropologie des Geschlechtslebens', in H. Giese (ed.), *Die Sexualität des Menschens*, Stuttgart, 1971, p. 4.

5 ibid.

6 K. Schneider attempts to overcome the difficulties involved in the assessment of deviant sexual behaviour by taking 'biological meaning' as his yardstick. 'Seen from this standpoint, everything that does not have procreation as its ultimate goal is strictly abnormal. And a sexual intention, a desire or an action is the more perverse, the more impossible it is that it should lead to procreation'. K. Schneider, *Klinische Psychopathologie*, Stuttgart, 1962, p. 160.

7 This is shown by a resolution of the Prussian supreme court in

1877. It was decided that 'paragraph 175 does not apply to indecent behaviour as such, but requires behaviour of a similar character to copulation, i.e. *an act seeking to satisfy the sexual desire in a similar manner to how this takes place in a natural fashion between persons of opposite sex*'. (Quoted from Günter Gollner, op. cit., p. 183; emphasis M.D.)

8 S. Ferenczi, 'The Nosology of Male Homosexuality (Homoeroticism)', in *First Contributions to Psycho-Analysis*, London, 1952, pp. 299-300.

9 ibid., p. 300.

10 ibid., p. 306.

11 Even if the German anti-homosexual legislation did not recognize Ferenczi's distinction, it is likely that the collective projections giving rise to the division of homosexuals into 'active' and 'passive' had their effect on the penalties imposed, and that 'active homosexuals' found more lenient judges.

3. *The Biologising of Ethics*

1 R. von Krafft-Ebing, *Psychopathia Sexualis; Sexual Aberration*, London, 1965, p. 56.

2 The following phenomena, among others, are adduced by Krafft-Ebing as a sign of homosexual sickness: 'The mental life of these men is frequently fanatically exaggerated.' 'In the majority of cases there are mental anomalies (outstanding talent for fine arts, especially music, poetry, etc.) together with intellectually poor gifts or general distortion.' 'Alongside the functional degeneracy symptom in the form of contrary sex-feeling there are often other kinds of functional and frequently, too, of anatomical, symptoms of degeneration.' loc. cit., pp. 318-19.

3 ibid., p. 318. Similar views were put forward by von Schrenck-Notzing, though he assumed a neuropathic disposition which required external influences in order to produce the sick homosexual orientation. See A. von Schrenck-Notzing, *Die Suggestionstherapie bei krankhaften Erscheinungen des Geschlechtssinnes mit besonderer Berücksichtigung der konträren Sexualempfindung*, Stuttgart, 1892.

4 I. Bloch, *Das Sexualleben unserer Zeit in seinen Beziehungen zur*

modernen Kultur, Berlin, 1907, p. 577. For all his insights, Bloch remained trapped in traditional ideas and viewed homosexuality as without meaning or purpose, since it went against the goals of the species: 'The mono- and homo-sexual instincts, restricted to the ego or the subject's own sex, are thus in their most profound nature *dys-teleological* and *anti-evolutionary*' (p. 592).

4. *An Alternative Anthropology*

1 The first published writings of C.H. Ulrichs appeared in the 1860s under the pseudonym Numa Numantius.
   [English translations of several of Ulrichs' works are now available from Urania Manuscripts, 1206 Hyperion Ave., Los Angeles, Ca. 90029, U.S.A.]

2 The collection of Ulrichs' works edited by Magnus Hirschfeld, *Forschungen über das Rätsel der mann-männlichen Liebe* (Leipzig, 1898), contains the following editorial dedication: 'To the eternal memory of Carl Heinrich Ulrichs on his centenary, the great champion who sacrificed himself for the liberation of lovers of their own sex from legal persecution and social contempt.' On Ulrichs' campaign for the liberation of homosexuals, see also the informative study by Jim Steakley, *The Homosexual Emancipation Movement in Germany*, 1975; and J. Lauritsen and D. Thorstad, *The Early Homosexual Rights Movement (1864-1935)*, New York, 1974.

3 C.H. Ulrichs, *Vindex*, Los Angeles, n.d. [1978], p. 4.

4 C.H. Ulrichs, *Inclusa*, Los Angeles, n.d. [1978], p. 63.

5 Hans Blüher, author of *The Role of Eroticism in Male Society* (1917), argued that male homoeroticism was the force underlying the political state. He sought to reinstate homosexuality, especially between men and boys, as an integral aspect of masculine behaviour. See Jim Steakley, op. cit., pp. 53-4. [Translator's note.]

6 C.H. Ulrichs, *Inclusa*, loc. cit., p. 31.

7 ibid.

8 Krafft-Ebing's classic work contains a note on Ulrichs which shows what little effect his ideas had on the medical establishment. 'In the mid-sixties of the 19th century there appeared a certain Judge *Ulrichs*, himself afflicted with this

perverse impulse, and proclaimed under the pen-name "Numa Numantius" in a number of writings that the mental sex-life is not bound up with bodily sex, that there were male individuals who felt themselves to be the wife of a man...*Ulrichs* was merely responsible for proving that this genuinely innate paradoxical sex-sentiment is a physiological phenomenon rather than a pathological one.' loc. cit., p. 320.

9 On this question see W.S. Schlegel, 'Homosexualität – ein soziales Ordnungsprinzip', in *Sexualmedizin* 8, 1973, pp. 296-8, and by the same author, *Die Sexualinstinkte des Menschen*, Munich, 1966, especially pp. 208 ff. Schlegel is criticised in M. Dannecker and R. Reiche, *Der gewöhnliche Homosexuelle*, loc. cit., pp. 27 ff. and 290.

10 R. Klimmer, *Die Homosexualität als biologisch-soziologische Zeitfrage*, Hamburg, 1965, pp. 282 ff.

11 An additional reason for pointing out this regression is to refute the crude conception of linear progress according to which the oppression of homosexuals is simply a precapitalist residue and gradually disappearing, an argument supported only by reference to the most recent legal reform.

12 See M. Hirschfeld, 'Ursachen und Wesen des Uranismus'. in *Jahrbuch für sexuelle Zwischenstufen*, 5, 1903, as well as his *Die Homosexualität des Mannes und des Weibes*, Berlin. 1920.

5. *Hirschfeld's Debate with Psychoanalysis*

1 S. Freud, Three Essays on the Theory of Sexuality'. *Standard Edition*, vol. 7, London, 1975, p. 145, note.

2 M. Hirschfeld, *Geschlechtskunde – auf Grunde dreissigjähriger Erfahrung und Forschung bearbeitet*, vol. 1, Stuttgart. 1926. p. 194.

3 Hirschfeld listed the following points: '1. The spontaneous... eruption of homoerotic sentiment. 2. The presence of difference already in childhood (specific traits of character, for example a girlish nature in boys and a boyish nature in girls). 3. The non-sexual subconscious attraction of the child to the later sexual object. 4. The non-existence of desire for the opposite sex. 5. The content of sexual dreams. 6. The agreement between sexual personality and sexual drive. 7. The possibility of recognising homosexuals by their physical

features. 8. The insusceptibility of homosexuality to external influence. 9. The parallel in all secondary phenomena between love for the other sex and for the same sex. 10. The appearance of homosexuality within the family. 11. The stable distribution of homosexuality irrespective of time and place. 12. A further proof for the innate character of homosexuality...is *"per exclusionem"*.' (op. cit., pp. 564 ff.)

4 ibid., p. 564.
5 S. Freud, op. cit., pp. 140-1.
6 Quoted from M. Hirschfeld, op. cit., p. 562.
7 ibid., p. 563.
8 E. Schorsch, 'Sexuelle Deviationen: Ideologie, Klinik, Kritik', in V. Sigusch (ed.), *Therapie sexueller Störungen*, p. 148.
9 *Bundestagsdrucksache IV/650*, loc. cit., p. 142.
10 R. Reiche, *Was heisst sexuelle Liberalisierung?*, an unpublished talk at the 11th Scientific Session of the Deutsche Gesellschaft für Sexualforschung, Hamburg, 1972.

6. *The Reduction of Homosexuality to the Homosexual*

1 Sandor Ferenczi provided certain key elements of a socio-psychological explanation for homophobia as early as 1914. He argued that the apparently increasing number of 'object homoerotics' was 'an abnormal reaction to the disproportionately exaggerated repression of the homoerotic instinct component by civilised man, i.e. a failure of this repression.' (op. cit., p. 314.) But if people are burdened by an excessive compulsion to repress the homosexual components of their libido, restricting their emotional and affectionate tendencies towards their own sex without however obliterating these, it is understandable why they are so full of hatred towards those who refuse to bow to this pressure. The hatred of homosexuals is thus a normal counterweight to the culturally induced and exaggerated repression of homoerotic libidinal components.
2 See note 3 to section 5.

7. *Psychoanalysis versus Sexology*

1 See for example S. Freud, 'Leonardo da Vinci and a Memory

of his Childhood', *Standard Edition*, vol. 11, London, 1971. p. 99, note.

2 'Three Essays on the Theory of Sexuality', *Standard Edition*, vol. 7, pp. 145-6, note.

3 I. Bloch, op. cit. p. 577.

4 S. Freud, 'Three Essays...', loc. cit., p. 146, note.

5 Hirschfeld, from his long experience of sexual research, was well aware of certain typical characteristics in the general personality of homosexuals. But he could see nothing more in these than a direct expression of the specific nature of the 'intermediate' type. Not only did he make the assumption, rejected by Freud, of an intimate association between sexual drive and sexual object. He also claimed that 'what is constitutional in homosexuality is most intimately linked with the whole being of the personality'. See M. Hirschfeld, *Geschlechtskunde...*, loc. cit., p. 567.

6 A. von Eulenburg's Preface to I. Bloch, *Beiträge zur Ätiologie der Psychopathia sexualis*, part 1, Dresden, 1902.

7 Cf. C.W. Socarides, *The Overt Homosexual*, New York, 1968.

8. *Anthropological Psychiatry*

1 I think the expression 'ethical anthropology' is justifiable, despite the assertion by H. Kunz that 'the intention, in acknowledging the norm as the necessary condition for perversion...is not any veiled attempt to judge the perversions in a moral or aesthetic sense and condemn them by their contravention of the norm' (H. Kunz, 'Zur Theorie der Perversion', in *Monatsschrift für Psychiatrie und Neurologie*, vol. 105, 1/2, 1942, p. 3). It is true that anthropological psychiatry more or less dispenses with any explicit sexual ethics. It can do this, however, because its ethics is already completely contained in its underlying assumption of the norm. According to Kunz, the norms that govern sexuality have a transhistorical validity: 'What remains decisive is the view that the norms which give order to interpersonal relations are primarily neither forms that have arisen socially and historically, nor are they primarily ethical ideals that undergo social and historical change; they are rather founded in the "social nature" of the human being itself' (ibid., p. 70).

This definition of the norm has no need to present an ethics of its own, for all those who do not accept the anthropological meaning of the norm are immoral by definition.

2 E. Strauss, 'Die Deformierung', in H. Giese (ed.), *Die sexuelle Perversion*, loc. cit., p. 191.

3 E. Schorsch, 'Psychopathologie der Sexualität', in H. Giese and E. Schorsch, *Zur Psychopathologie der Sexualität*, Stuttgart, 1973, pp. 10 ff.

4 Anthropological psychiatry does not abandon the idea of perversion as sickness. Rather, it expands the concept of sickness into the social sphere, so that the 'sickness' of sexual perversion is endowed with as it were epidemic features.

5 H. Kunz, op. cit., p. 70.

6 ibid.

7 Gehlen also agrees with anthropological psychiatry in rejecting an explicit ethics. As Wolf Lepenies points out, he can do without this because 'his theory of institutions and his concept of the human being as a "domestic animal" already contain it in full'. (See Wolf Lepenies, 'Anthropologie als Gesellschaftskritik', in W. Lepenies et al, *Kritik der Anthropologie*, Munich, 1971, p. 82).

8 See A. Gehlen, *Der Mensch – Seine Natur und seine Stellung in der Welt* (10th edition), Frankfurt, 1974.

9 H. Schelsky's *Soziologie der Sexualität* is completely in the tradition of Gehlen's anthropology, and would have been inconceivable without it.

10 H. Schelsky, *Soziologie der Sexualität*, Hamburg, 1955, p. 62.

11 ibid.

12 ibid.

13 According to Marcuse, the perversions 'express rebellion against the subjugation of sexuality under the order of procreation, and against the institutions which guarantee this order' (H. Marcuse, *Eros and Civilisation*, New York, 1962, p. 45).

14 Gehlen depicts the results of institutional breakdown, the decay of humanity into a dreaded 'state of nature', completely in the tenor of the psychiatric phenomenology of the perversions: 'If the external guarantees and stabilising forces that are rooted in firm traditions decay and are undermined, our behaviour is then deformed, governed by emotion, impulsive, incalculable and unreliable.' (A. Gehlen,

'Das Bild des Menschens im Lichte der modernen Anthropologie', in *Anthropologische Forschung*, Reinbek, 1972, p. 59.)

9. *The Wave of Liberalism*

1 The influence of Kinsey was a key one, his theory doing away with everything specific in the distinction between heterosexuality and homosexuality.

2 Hirschfeld took several pages to list the actual or supposed distinctions between homosexuals and heterosexuals. He ended up: 'Out of 1,500 homosexuals, I have not seen one who is not both mentally and physically distinct from the normal man, and I therefore will not believe in the existence of such until I have personally met him.' (M. Hirschfeld, *Ursachen und Wesen des Uranismus*, loc. cit., p. 86; see also pp. 79 ff.)

3 See H. Giese, *Der homosexuelle Mann in der Welt*, Munich, n.d.

4 V.E. von Gebsattel, 'Prolegomena einer medizinischen Anthropologie', in *Ausgewählte Aufsätze*, Berlin, 1954, p. 161.

5 ibid., p. 164.

6 H. Kunz, 'Zur Theorie der Perversionen', loc. cit., p. 43.

7 On Giese's work see also M. Dannecker and R. Reiche, *Der gewöhnliche Homosexuelle*, loc. cit., pp. 156 ff.

8 Such considerations are voiced by Rüdiger Lautmann, who believes that the unintended result of social research aimed at disclosing deviant phenomena is 'the reinforcement of existing prejudices and stigmatisation'. R. Lautmann, 'Stigma Homosexualität', in *Sexualmedizin* 9, 1974, p. 445.

9 R. Klimmer, op. cit., p. 273.

10 More or less clear evidence of differences such as these is presented throughout the empirical survey by R. Reiche and myself, *Der gewöhnliche Homosexuelle*, loc. cit.

10. *The Popular 'Attitude' To Homosexuals*

1 On this subject see 'Die homosexuelle Berufsbiographie' in M. Dannecker and R. Reiche, *Der gewöhnliche Homosexuelle*, loc. cit., pp. 325 ff.

2 *Presse-Information* 8/1974 of the Gesellschaft zur Förderung

sozialwissenschaftlicher Sexualforschung, Düsseldorf, 1974.

3 ibid.

4 On this subject see 'Der Homosexuellen-Hass der Homo-sexuellen', in M. Dannecker and R. Reiche, op. cit., pp. 351 ff.

5 There is a detailed description and analysis of the homosexual subculture in M. Dannecker and R. Reiche, op. cit., pp. 93 ff.

6 The bars, in particular, which differ from other 'public' sectors of the homosexual subculture in that, despite the casual character of the sexual contacts they facilitate, they do require a rather greater degree of interaction with the prospective sexual partner, are losing their preeminent position. Following the American example, bars are now being established in Germany, too, with a murky back-room where people can get down to business right away.

7 This violent separation is not just characteristic of the subculture, but affects each individual homosexual, as according to the milieu in which he finds himself he is either just a homosexual or not a homosexual, and in both cases equally diminished. On the one hand, this is expressed in the way that the homosexual aspect is excluded in certain sectors of society. Since homosexuals cannot necessarily be recognised as such and need not give themselves away, they are most often taken for heterosexuals, and even forced to join in the crude talk about women, with behaviour to match, characteristic of all-male situations and deriving from the sexual desires and compulsive representations of hetero-sexuality.

Such grotesque situations can arise here as that recounted to me by a gay man working in the fashion trade. He found himself accompanying some of his customers on a business trip to an Asian country where prostitutes are supposedly cheap and available. At all events his fellow-travellers, though married, persuaded the man to visit with them an appropriate establishment. Being in high spirits and raring to go, they soon found their homosexual friend a suitable woman, despite his understandable reservations. Everyone went to their respective rooms. But because even homosexuality doesn't prevent you from being stupid, the unhappy young man still couldn't bring himself to explain to his companion the reason for his lack of interest. This only led to more trouble. Though she'd been paid in advance, the woman insisted on consummating the deal, and it was only with difficulty that he managed to fend her off. And yet this didn't prevent him from having a proper story to tell the next morning, so he could join in the general sexual bragging.

In the subcultural milieu, on the other hand, the reduction to being just a homosexual is scarcely less violent, and something of this violence remains even in the attempts made to escape it. Since this social division insinuates itself as simply part of the natural order of things, the only option for those unable to accept it is to forcibly introduce the excluded side into the situation.

11. *The Specific Homosexual Biography*

1 Here I can only refer to Rüdiger Lautmann's essay 'Stigma Homosexualität' and not to his later and longer work which appeared only after I had finished the present book. I still believe, though, that the essential points of my critique of a research inspired by labelling theory apply equally to Lautmann's later work. (See R. Lautmann, 'Kontrolle durch Pathologisierung', in R. Lautmann (ed.), *Seminar: Gesellschaft und Homosexualität*, Frankfurt, 1977.)

2 R. Lautmann, 'Stigma Homosexualität', in *Sexualmedizin* 3, 1974, p. 445.

3 ibid.

4 On this subject see T. Brocher, *Benachteiligte Gruppen in der Gesellschaft – Homosexuelle*, manuscript of a radio talk broadcast on 4 June 1972.

5 E.M. Lemert, 'Der Begriff des sekundären Devianz', in K. Lüdersen and F. Sack (eds), *Seminar: Abweichendes Verhalten I – Die selektiven Normen der Gesellschaft*, Frankfurt, 1975, p. 436.

6 See R. Lautmann, 'Stigma Homosexualität', loc. cit., p. 444.

7 A detailed depiction of the coming-out process is given in M. Dannecker and R. Reiche, op. cit., pp. 23 ff. [Here and elsewhere, Martin Dannecker uses the term 'coming out' in a wider sense than is usual in English; he means the whole process of self-awareness, the development of a gay lifestyle and the struggle for social acceptance. – Translator.]

8 See on this point the clinical history published in connection

with a controversy between H. Blüher and J. Sadger; H. Blüher, 'Studien über den perversen Charakter', in H. Giese (ed.), *Die sexuelle Perversion*, loc. cit., pp. 101 ff.

9 R. Lautmann, 'Stigma Homosexualität', loc. cit., p. 445.

10 See H. Giese and G. Schmidt, *Studenten-Sexualität*, Reinbek, 1968, p. 145.

11 G. Schmidt and V. Sigusch, *Arbeiter-Sexualität*, Berlin, 1971, p. 127.

12 On this point see M. Dannecker and R. Reiche, op. cit., pp. 236 ff.

13 S. Schäfer and G. Schmidt, *Weibliche Homosexualität. Dokumentation der Ergebnisse einer Untersuchung an homosexuellen und bisexuellen Frauen in der BRD.* (Unpublished MS., Hamburg, 1973.)

14 The comparison is between 151 homosexual women between 18 and 35, and 581 homosexual men between 16 and 35.

15 See S. Schäfer, 'Sociosexual Behavior in Male and Female Homosexuals. A Study in Sex Differences', in *Archives of Sexual Behavior*, vol. 6, 5, 1977, pp. 355-64.

16 Compare the corresponding data for heterosexual women in S. Schäfer, op. cit., p. 361.

17 According to the results obtained by Reimut Reiche and myself, a fifth of those who had steady relationships 'often' had sexual contacts with other men, and a half did so 'sometimes'. (op. cit., p. 178).

18 ibid., pp. 182 ff.

19 M.S. Weinberg and C.J. Williams, *Male Homosexuals – Their Problems and Adaptations*, New York, 1974.

20 ibid, p. 178.

21 The most important distinction made between the European countries and the USA was the presence or absence of legal penalities for homosexual behaviour. The popular attitude in the societies in question was also taken into account. According to these factors, anti-homosexual repression in the USA is significantly stronger than in Holland or Denmark.

22 M.S. Weinberg and C.J. Williams, op. cit., p. 88.

23 ibid.

24 Conditions in Holland have long shown how a thriving subculture can only grow up in a liberal social atmosphere. The tolerance expressed in the great number of clubs, bars, saunas, etc. exerted a magical attraction on very many

homosexuals from countries with a more repressive climate
and correspondingly fewer subcultural facilities, which in
turn led to a further growth.

25 M. Hoffman, *Die Welt der Homosexuellen*, Frankfurt, 1971, p.
132.

26 M.S. Weinberg and C.J. Williams, op. cit., p. 162.

27 ibid., p. 179.

12. *Deviance and Social Adaptation*

1 R. Lautmann, 'Stigma Homosexualität', loc. cit., p. 443.

2 Klaus Horn pertinently characterised the labelling approach
as 'the sociological substitute for psychology'. See K. Horn,
'Psychoanalyse und gesellschaftliche Widersprüche', in
Psyche, vol. 30, p. 46.

3 H.S. Becker, *Aussenseiter – Zur Soziologie abweichenden
Verhaltens*, Frankfurt, 1973. p. 13.

4 'I believe...that social groups create deviant behaviour by
setting up rules which deviant behaviour is defined in terms of
breaking, and that they apply these rules to certain peole
whom they label as outsiders.' (H.S. Becker, op. cit., p. 18.)

5 ibid., p. 13.

6 This aspect of a thoroughly negative or at best benignly
neutral reaction comes through particularly clearly in an
attempt by John I. Kitsuse to apply the model of interaction
theory to homosexuals and confirm it empirically. It is true
that the cases studied by Kitsuse rarely showed extreme
negative reactions in the sphere of everyday interaction, but
neither could there by any unrestrainedly positive reactions
when the attitude of heterosexuals to the sexual interests of
their interactors was also taken into account. Even in those
encounters where nothing dramatic followed the identification of the other actor as a homosexual, the incongruence of
sexual needs was still there, and so the end of the interaction
procedure was still followed by rejection, as comes through in
the examples Kitsuse describes. See J.I. Kitsuse, 'Societal
Reaction to Deviant Behaviour', in E. Rubington and M.S.
Weinberg (eds), *Deviance – The Interactionist Perspective*, New
York, 1973, pp. 16-25.

7 In Kitsuse's study, the past aspect and the aspect of difference

come through all the time in the interaction between 'non-conformers' (homosexuals) and 'conformers' (heterosexuals), but this is never treated as a specific theme. Kitsuse greets with astonishment the fact that people mutually interpret and identify one another in their interaction. He particularly stresses in connection with labelling that the heterosexuals questioned observed something strange or unusual about their interactor either before or after identifying him or her as homosexual. In fact the encounters Kitsuse describes show many features that are quite remarkable from the heterosexual standpoint. For instance, a chance meeting between a college student and a homosexual man in a café ended with the latter offering to take the student by taxi 40 blocks to Times Square. It is scarcely surprising that such an offer should be interpreted as unusual, and having some ulterior motive behind it; after all, it doesn't happen every day. The outcome was predictable: the homosexual used the journey to signal his interest in no uncertain terms, and the student was equally clear in his rejection.

This particular episode is trivial, and has nothing specifically homosexual about it. But it is characteristic precisely in its triviality, or rather in the duplication of the triviality by Kitsuse. It is certainly one of the merits of interaction theory, with its weakness for the trivial, that it has exposed many everyday phenomena as in fact stigmatising. The scientific treatment of the trivial, however, should not fall behind that of much maligned common sense. Common sense at least interprets whatever it finds strange or unusual, or it certainly tries to do so. It proceeds in the same way even when it has not yet been able to identify the strangeness in question. Through this subsequent identification what had appeared strange and unusual is illuminated, and there is at least a partial understanding of the possibilities of dealing with it in an appropriate way. If this procedure contains a labelling element, it is impossible to assume that this is purely arbitrary. What is happening here at the everyday level is the same as happens at the level of conceptual thought, if in a different way and in a less concentrated form. The dilemma of labelling theory is that it cannot manage without labels itself (and strictly speaking it is already a stigmatising label to use the adjective or noun 'homosexual'), despite its radical aversion to labels and its refusal to distinguish between true labels and false.

8 It may be that H.S. Becker's theory is more applicable to other groups of 'social outsiders' than it is to homosexuals. The reason why the very approach of labelling theory is so unfruitful is the case of homosexual behaviour is that it starts with a 'choice between various contrary modes of behaviour' (Becker, op. cit., p. 53), setting the social constraints too high and the mental constraints too low: 'Confronted for the first time with the consequences of his action, which may be extremely drastic, it is still possible for the person to decide that he doesn't want to tread the path of deviance and turn back. If he makes the right choice, he is accepted back into the conventional community; but if he makes the wrong choice he is rejected, and the cycle of increasingly deviant behaviour sets in' (Becker, op. cit.). Homosexuals, however, have no such freedom of choice. It is not up to a homosexual to decide whether he is to become so or not. If manifest homosexuality did depend on voluntary decision in this way, it is probable that a quite significant section of homosexuals would opt for conventional heterosexuality. Once you are homosexual, the most you can decide is to refrain from sexual activity. But even the abstinent homosexual is still more like a practising homosexual than a heterosexual, as far as his position as outsider is concerned.

9 Guy Hocquenghem, loc. cit., p. 36.

13. *Homosexuality as a Psychological Phenomenon*

1 F. Morgenthaler, op. cit., p. 1079.
2 ibid. In contrast to Morgenthaler, Socarides is unable to discover any progressive aspect in homosexuality, and interprets it simply as a regressive adaptation. See C.W. Socarides, *The Overt Homosexual*, loc. cit.
3 F. Morgenthaler, op. cit., p. 1085.
4 On this point see M. Dannecker and R. Reiche, *Der gewöhnliche Homosexuelle*, loc. cit., pp. 347 ff.
5 F. Morgenthaler, op. cit., p. 1081.
6 ibid.
7 ibid, and pp. 1081 ff.

8 ibid., p. 1083.

9 ibid. Of the homosexuals questioned by R. Reiche and myself, 25% had at some time in their lives 'visited a doctor, psychologist, psychiatrist or some other person professionally concerned with human problems'. Only about 20% of this group had undertaken any prolonged treatment. (See M. Dannecker and R. Reiche, op. cit., p. 361.)

10 While Socarides simply extrapolates his clinical experience with homosexual patients suffering accute and serious disturbances to homosexuals in general, believing that 'every homosexual, both male and female, lives this close to the brink of personal disaster and possible annihilation' (C.W. Socarides, op. cit., p. 45), so that he must really be surprised why so few become patients, Morgenthaler comes to the opposite conclusion. He seems to believe that all those whose suffering is great enough will spontaneously decide to seek psychotherapeutic help, so that the rest must be more or less healthy. It seems highly likely that both views are seriously wrong in their assessment of the level of mental disorders among homosexuals, though in opposite directions.

11 O.F. Kernberg, 'Barriers to Falling and Remaining in Love', in *Journal of the American Psychoanalytic Association*, vol. 22, 3, 1974, p. 509.

12 Only some 6% of homosexual men have the kind of long-term exclusive relationship that would meet Kernberg's criterion of normality. At the other extreme, about 11% have either never had any love relationship, or not in the past 5 years. (M. Dannecker and R. Reiche, op. cit., pp. 180 ff. & 158 ff.). These findings can of course give only a vague idea. It is nearly impossible with an empirical investigation, especially one based on a questionnaire, to reach any firm conclusions as to the quality of a sexual relationship. Unconscious regions that find expression in relations with the partner would have to be drawn into the analysis. Being forced to stick to the most general and crude criteria, such as duration, sexual contacts, etc., what we get is usually little more than the facade of things.It may well be, then, that the category 'enduring and passionate relationship' also includes individuals who, on closer investigation, could not be immediately classed as capable of love. It may also be that those who behave promiscuously for year after year without getting into a

relationship have other reasons for this than an incapacity for love, though this is rather less likely.

13 O.F. Kernberg, op. cit., p. 488.

14 ibid., p. 510.

15 S. Freud, 'Fragment of an Analysis of a Case of Hysteria', *Standard Edition*, vol. 7, London, 1975, p. 43.

16 F. Morgenthaler, op. cit., p. 1093.

17 'Homosexuality thus serves to protect the personality against regression. If homosexual behaviour did not occur the patient would proceed to the extreme of regression which would lead to a reinstating of the undifferentiated phase with loss of ego boundaries and dissolution of self.' (C.W. Socarides, op. cit., p. 64.)

18 Morgenthaler fails to distinguish sufficiently between homosexuality and the perversions. Yet even where homosexuals are not specifically mentioned, his fundamental findings apply to them too.

19 F. Morgenthaler, op. cit., p. 1092.

21 'Homosexuals desperately need and seek a contact whenever they feel weakened, frightened, deprived, guilty, ashamed or in any way helpless or powerless', in Socarides' description of this process (op. cit., p. 63).

21 F. Morgenthaler, op. cit., p. 1080.

22 ibid., p. 1094.

23 On this point see M. Dannecker and R. Reiche, op. cit., p. 162. Weinberg and Williams' study also shows a connection between high homosexual activity and higher or stable self-esteem. All of the factors they investigate that have any bearing on homosexual self-esteem point in this direction. When homosexual frequency is high, so too is the share of those with an adequate self-esteem. This is true with all three groups studied, in the USA, Holland and Denmark. The trend is especially impressive among those whom Weinberg and Williams class as 'highly depressive':

Homosexual Frequency

	high	medium	low
High depression			
USA	19.3%	36.2%	45.3%
Holland	22.7%	40.5%	50.5%
Denmark	29.2%	39.1%	66.7%

See Weinberg and Williams, op. cit., p. 167.

24 F. Morgenthaler, op. cit., p. 1090.

14. *The Superior Homosexual*

1 Guy Hocquenghem, op. cit., p. 117.
2 ibid.
3 Despite my belief that homosexuals can indeed have happy, passionate and lasting relationships, the specific character of these must be stressed. What makes them successful cannot be assessed in terms of traditional ideas of the couple. Rather than the duration of the relationship, which need not be for ever, more important factors are mutual understanding of the basic problems that a relationship can throw up, and an understanding that does not stop short when faced with 'sexual infidelity'. For this and other reasons a homosexual relationship cannot be assessed in terms of the traditional notions of love and fidelity.
4 'Homosexual encounters do not take place in the seclusion of a domestic setting but outside, in the open air, in forests and on beaches' (Guy Hocquenghem, op. cit., p. 117).
5 It is impossible in the context of this book to trace the connecting lines between Hocquenghem's essay and Deleuze and Guattari's *Anti-Oedipus*. But these are extremely dense, and Hocquenghem's essay would be hard to conceive of without *Anti-Oedipus* behind it. (G. Deleuze and F. Guattari, *Anti-Oedipe*, Paris, 1972.)
6 G. Hocquenghem, op. cit., pp. 117-8. (Emphasis M. D.)
7 ibid., p. 117.

Gay Men's Press is an independent publishing project set up to produce books relevant to the male gay movement and to promote the ideas of gay liberation. Our catalogue and books are available from:
Gay Men's Press,
27 Priory Avenue,
London N8 7RN,
England.
For mail orders, add 30p. per copy.

If you found this book interesting, you may enjoy another title in our list that discusses gay male psychology in a very different way:

Mario Mieli   UK £3.95/US $8.95
Homosexuality and Liberation:
elements of a gay critique

A scathing freudo-marxist attack on heterosexual society by a founder of the Italian gay movement. 'Mieli's anger, outrageousness and uniquely gay sense of humour draw the reader into the passion of gay strength and militancy' *(Gay Community News)*. 'A classic of gay liberation literature' *(Gay News)*. 'An excellent introduction to the dialogue with Freudianism' *(Advocate)*. 'Mario Mieli is a Marcuse in drag, a Tantric acid-queen politico. . . the strongest male contribution to sexual politics theory I know of' *(Undercurrents)*.

Daniel Tsang (ed.)   UK £3.25/US $5.95[*]
The Age Taboo:
gay male sexuality, power and consent

A collection of writings from a variety of standpoints on the controversial topic of man/boy love. With contributions by Tom Reeves, *Gay Left*, Tom O'Carroll, Kate Millett, Roger Moody, *Lesbians Rising*, Joint Council for Gay Teenagers and many more.

Mario Dubsky   UK £4.95/US $9.95
Tom Pilgrim's Progress Among the Consequences of Christianity and other drawings; introduced by Edward Lucie-Smith
A collection of 65 drawings which develop the tradition of the male nude in a modern perspective, or explore the shadowy sides of myth. The 'Tom Pilgrim' sequence was prompted by the blasphemy trial against the London *Gay News*.

In an introductory essay the leading art critic Edward Lucie-Smith discusses Mario Dubsky's work and the concept of gay art.

David Fernbach   UK £3.75/US $6.95[*]
The Spiral Path: a gay contribution to human survival

What has gay liberation to do with environmental pollution or the threat of nuclear war? A dissident communist presents the struggle against the gender system as central to human survival and evolution. This discussion will stimulate debate throughout the field of radical politics.

Richard Dipple (ed.)   UK £2.50/US $5.50
Cracks in the Image: stories by gay men
'Vivid authenticity of presentation. The Gay Life as she is lived. There will be few readers who won't find themselves in at least one of the miniatures' *(Gay News)*.

Heinz Heger   UK £2.50/US $4.95*
The Men With the Pink Triangle
A unique personal memoir of the life and death of homosexual prisoners under Nazi persecution. 'A moving example of the will to "bear witness" on the part of people who survived the death camps' *(Times Literary Supplement)*.

Noël Greig and Drew Griffiths UK £2.50/US $5.50
Two Gay Sweatshop Plays (As Time Goes By and The Dear Love of Comrades)
The two most acclaimed productions of the Gay Sweatshop men's company, on the themes of gay history and the life of Edward Carpenter. 'Between these covers lie two outstanding achievements' *(Gay News)*.

Rosa von Praunheim   UK £3.95/US $8.95
Army of Lovers
Interviews with prominent figures in the US gay movement — the book of the film. 'A brainstorming of questions to take us into the Eighties' *(Body Politic)*.

Aubrey Walter (ed.)   UK £3.95/US $8.95
Come Together: the years of gay liberation 1970-73
Tells the story of the beginnings of the Gay Liberation movement in Britain: 'the excitement of a time when human consciousness was making a quantum jump' *(Gay News)*.

*Books marked with an asterisk are published separately in North America by Alyson Publications, PO Box 2783, Boston, Mass. 02208, USA. North American readers can also order other Gay Men's Press titles from this address. For mail orders, please add $.75 per copy.

David Rees　　　　　　　　UK £2.50/US $4.95
The Milkman's On His Way

Teenager Ewan Macrae is a milkman's son from Cornwall.
The author of gay best-seller *In the Tent* tells of Ewan's
search for a gay identity with a sensitive frankness that is
long awaited in a novel for young people.

Alan Bray　　　　　　　　UK £2.95/US $5.95
Homosexuality in Renaissance England

Charts how the transition England experienced between
1550 and 1700 affected the position of homosexuality.
From the medieval view of 'sodomy' as a vice which
anyone could fall prey to, the first signs of a separate
homosexual subculture gradually become visible.

Ian Everton　　　　　　　　UK £2.95/US $5.95
Alienation

A novel of the British gay movement. In a Northern city a
gay group battle against a homophobic society. The
arrival of a new member, lost and suffering from amnesia,
throws the unresolved contradictions in their own ranks
into sharp perspective.